MUSIC
ON THE
WIND

Meditations and Prayers
based on the life of David

by Eddie Askew

By the same author:

A Silence and A Shouting
Disguises of Love
Many Voices One Voice
No Strange Land
Facing the Storm
Breaking the Rules
Cross Purposes
Slower than Butterflies

© The Leprosy Mission International
80 Windmill Road, Brentford
Middlesex TW8 0QH, UK

© Paintings and drawings A. D. (Eddie) Askew

A. D. (Eddie) Askew has asserted his right to be identified
as the author of this book.

Published 1998
A catalogue record for this book is available from the British Library

ISBN 0 902731 40 8

*To Georgia Grace whose appearance
coincided with the writing of this book
and who has graced our lives with love.*

Paintings and drawings by the author

Foreword

When I heard that Eddie Askew had a new book in mind, I was delighted for his use of imagery has enriched many peoples' lives. I knew that Eddie would not dodge the issues of life if he looked at someone like King David. I also knew that I would get some new psalms for Eddie's writing is often lyrical. In all this I am not disappointed; *Music on the Wind* is a rich source of prayer in the very fullness of life.

We start with 'Dreams' and the need to have 'bright visions of a finer world'. But we are not only to dream dreams but to strive for their fulfilment. We are asked to 'Face Reality' - 'even - especially - when the tide's run out and I am beached in doubt'. Again and again we are asked to direct our gaze to the eternal that is ever in our midst; to shake off the need for role playing and be who we are called to be.

From 'Facing Reality' where would you expect to go but to 'Broken Dreams', broken hopes and broken promises. There is no doubt that we all fail to live up to our ideals and hopes. We need to learn to live with pain, agony and tragedy for they are part of the human lot. But so is the transforming presence and abiding love of God, and we must not let the dark images destroy the reality. Even if we lose our grip of God, He does not lose His hold on us.

This is all very nice, but the desert encroaches and sometimes, like on the day of the crucifixion, it seems there is no answer to our 'why's'. There are times of darkness and of thirsting after God. We need to learn to wait and to trust. Even more we need to discover that 'you'll be there on the road with me'.

In the final movement, because David is human, we are faced with 'full frontal temptation', passion, the fire of God and the healing flame. Every facet of life has been faced, and often full on, and out of this turbulence has come new songs. There is a deeper discovery, 'the tune I play is yours. There all the time if only I had listened'.

Eddie has listened to the *Music on the Wind*. If you listen to what he has heard, you will learn 'to sing and make music to the Lord in your heart'.

Rev Canon David Adam

Holy Island

Contents

Introduction

On the desk in front of me lies a small bronze dagger. It's covered in the rich green patina that comes from lying under the ground in the Middle East for about three thousand years before it was excavated. It was fashioned around the time of King David. It has no voice but it speaks to me. As I hold it, my mind reaches out in imagination to the period when David was struggling to survive, sometimes against his own king, Saul, more often against the Iron Age invaders, the Philistines. It is a tangible contact with the past and in a strange way it brings David to life.

This book is not a biography of David. It is an exercise in imagination based on his story. It is selective. Some people may find that I've left out events they believe are important, but in a small book choices have to be made. I had difficulty with the grammar of the book. David was, is, so real and immediate that I kept putting verbs in the present tense as though I was commenting on the story as it happened.

For busy people I have included the basic Bible quotations, but it is well worth taking the time to read the whole of David's story in the First and Second Books of Samuel.

David's story is one of a lifelong encounter with God. Sometimes the music of God's presence comes to David gently like the liquid notes of a shepherd's flute on a soft breeze, soothing and easy to hear. David responds and seeks to capture some of the music in his own.

At other times the breeze turns to storm, the music to symphony, building to the glory of a great crescendo that crashes and reverberates around David, God's presence echoing through every hidden corner of his life, impossible to ignore.

There are silences too. Intervals when God seems to withdraw to the edge of David's life and waits for David to make the first move, the first hesitant step, towards him. No music can be heard, only the sound of stillness stretching out bleakly in the wind drop quiet.

These are the most difficult movements in life but they can become the most productive. They are the *in between times*, the Easter Saturdays, the times of waiting when nothing seems to be happening; but they are seasons of preparation, the pause between death and resurrection, periods of great significance 'At the still point of the turning world' as T. S. Elliot describes them.

On occasion David no longer listens. The clamour of his own desires drowns out the music, turns harmony into discord. But whether he listens or not, God's music plays on, its variations forming and reforming, drawing David nearer, weaving the melody of his life phrase by phrase into the pattern of God's own until David becomes one with the music, and he realises that the music was playing within him all the time.

Eddie Askew

August 1998

Part One

Dreams

Reading : 1 Samuel 16:1 - 13

The Lord said to Samuel, 'How long will you mourn for Saul, since I have rejected him as king over Israel? Fill your horn with oil and be on your way; I am sending you to Jesse of Bethlehem. I have chosen one of his sons to be king.'

But Samuel said, 'How can I go? Saul will hear about it and kill me.'

The Lord said, 'Take a heifer with you and say, "I have come to sacrifice to the Lord." Invite Jesse to the sacrifice, and I will show you what to do. You are to anoint for me the one I indicate.'

Samuel did what the Lord said. When he arrived at Bethlehem, the elders of the town trembled when they met him. They asked, 'Do you come in peace?'

Samuel replied, 'Yes, in peace; I have come to sacrifice to the Lord. Consecrate yourselves and come to the sacrifice with me.' Then he consecrated Jesse and his sons and invited them to the sacrifice.

When they arrived, Samuel saw Eliab and thought, 'Surely the Lord's anointed stands here before the Lord.'

But the Lord said to Samuel, 'Do not consider his appearance or his height, for I have rejected him. The Lord does not look at the things man looks at. Man looks at the outward appearance, but the Lord looks at the heart.'

Then Jesse called Abinadab and made him pass in front of Samuel. But Samuel said, 'The Lord has not chosen this one either.' Jesse then made Shammah pass by, but Samuel said, 'Nor has the Lord chosen this one.' Jesse made seven of his sons pass before Samuel, but Samuel said to him, 'The Lord has not chosen these.' So he asked Jesse, 'Are these all the sons you have?'

'There is still the youngest,' Jesse answered, 'but he is tending the sheep.'

Samuel said, 'Send for him; we will not sit down until he arrives.'

So he sent and had him brought in. He was ruddy, with a fine appearance and handsome features.

Then the Lord said, 'Rise and anoint him; he is the one.'

So Samuel took the horn of oil and anointed him in the presence of his brothers, and from that day on the Spirit of the Lord came upon David in power. Samuel then went to Ramah.

Driving the Sheep

Imagine

Imagine a grassy hillside in Spring. It's warm in the sun and the grass is dotted with flowers, golden yellow, white, and the vivid scarlet of anemones and wild tulips. The hillside is scored by narrow tracks following the contours of the ground, paths worn by generations of sheep grazing over the centuries. Overhead a hawk hovers almost motionless in the blue sky, held on the invisible up-currents of warm air.

Behind us is a scatter of flat-roofed village houses, the poorer ones mud-walled, others substantial in stone. The only sounds we hear are the ordinary sounds of the countryside. The cry of a bird alarmed by the hawk, the distant bleating of sheep. The bark of a dog and the cry of a shepherd muted by distance as he calls to another across the valley.

The smells are country smells too. The odour of sheep and crushed grass; and sweat as we climb the slope in the sun, the breeze gentle on our faces. Just an ordinary day.

Then we hear a new sound. It's music, the liquid sound of a lyre, the notes cascading gently up and down the scale, carried on the soft wind. It's a simple melody, experimental, tentative, changing. We follow the sound around the hillside, and there, with his back to a rock in the shade of a scrubby tree, a young man sits.

He's sturdy, handsome, tanned brown by outdoor life. He wears a simple grey woollen gown, spun from the fleece of the family sheep and coarse woven at home. It's pulled back around his knees, and near his bare feet lies a pair of worn leather sandals. He's David.

We watch him quietly as he plays. His sheep are scattered over the hillside but he can see them. Most anyway. After a few more notes he puts the lyre down, stands up, stretches, and calls to the sheep. They hear his voice, know that he's near.

He picks up a stone, hefts it in his hand to test its weight, then pulls a leather sling from his belt. Eyeing a small bush twenty yards away, he whirls the sling around his head and lets fly. A hit. He tries again, this time aiming at a small rock further away. His sling stone hits accurate and hard, bouncing high with its force.

He sits down and after a few minutes he begins to tap out a rhythm on the ground with his stick, then picks up his lyre again. This time as he begins to play his lips move. We edge nearer to listen. The words aren't very clear at first, but he's singing something about sheep and shepherds.

He repeats it all several times, committing it to memory because he has no paper and anyway he can't read or write. He'll need to polish it before he can share it with anyone else, but it's the beginning of a new song to his God. 'The Lord is my shepherd . . .'

Psalm 23

The Lord is my shepherd, I shall not be in want.
He makes me lie down in green pastures,
he leads me beside quiet waters,
he restores my soul.
He guides me in paths of righteousness for his name's sake.
Even though I walk
through the valley of the shadow of death,
I will fear no evil,
for you are with me;
your rod and your staff,
they comfort me.

You prepare a table before me
in the presence of my enemies.
You anoint my head with oil;
my cup overflows.
Surely goodness and love will follow me
all the days of my life,
and I will dwell in the house of the Lord for ever.

Quiet Waters

When he [Samuel] arrived at Bethlehem, the elders of the town trembled when they met him. They asked, 'Do you come in peace?' 1 Samuel 16:4

The writer of *Gentle Jesus, meek and mild* has a lot to answer for. It may be a reassuring image for the crèche, but not for the mature Christian. I've never had much sympathy with the idea that Christians should be professional doormats, constantly giving way and inviting people to walk over them. True, Jesus spoke about turning the other cheek, but he also drove traders from the Temple.

The prophet Samuel is no poodle. Under God he is his own man. Tough, at times even violent. That may be hard to stomach but he was a man of his times, and the times were turbulent. We'd find him hard to live with, but God worked through him as he did through David, and neither of them was allergic to a good battle when it was needed.

Samuel faced hard decisions with courage and, when he needed to, spoke out strongly whatever the consequences. So the elders trembled when he appeared in the town and hoped it would be a peaceful visit. It was, although I doubt if they were able to relax fully until they'd seen him leave.

The crucial issue for me is to know when to be tough and when to give way. I'm not keen on confrontation anyway and, although I recognise its necessity at times, I like to keep it as a last resort. The judgement calls for a lifetime's experience and that often comes too late to help. 'How is it you don't make many mistakes?' asked the young man. 'That's experience,' said the elder. 'How do I get experience?' asked the young man. 'By making mistakes,' came the answer.

Maybe though, one indicator we see in Jesus' life is that when he was angry it was on behalf of other people facing injustice or hypocrisy, and when it was only his own toes that were being trodden on he kept his cool. That seems to be a good pattern to live by.

Do you come in peace, Lord?
I'd like to think so,
but there are times
when you disturb more than you comfort.
Times when you ask for things
I'm not prepared to give
and faced with your demands
I want to run for cover,
hide,
and wait for you to go away.

I tell myself I'm seeking peace
but I've a strong suspicion
that I'm really looking
for a bit of quiet.
And that's a very different thing.

I'd love a place where I could sit,
indulge myself,
and let the world go by.
A chance to turn my back on life
and paint reality
in comfortable colours.
A palatable palette of my own choice.

The trouble is
that when I think
I've got it organised,
I find your elbows digging hard
into the ribs of my complacency,
leaving me sore.
I'd ask a little gentleness from you
but something tells me
that's not what I need.
The occasional prod
is more appropriate,
reminding me that life is meant for living,
and opting out is not an option I can take.

Lord, help me realise
that whatever life may bring today
it comes wrapped up in you.
And that should be enough.

'Consecrate yourselves and come to the sacrifice with me.' 1 Samuel 16:5

Samuel demands that the people prepare themselves for God's service. Looking back in the Old Testament, consecration was about cleanliness, getting ready to enter God's presence by bathing and putting on clean clothes. Maybe there's a gentle echo today in the way some folk still stress the importance of dressing up to go to church. No bad thing, but not an essential.

There's a deeper significance to it though, one which David sang about later, and which must have been developing within his thoughts as his relationship with God grew more perceptive.

> *'Who may ascend the hill of the Lord?*
> *Who may stand in his holy place?*
> *He who has clean hands and a pure heart . . .'* (Psalm 24:3 - 4).

If David were alive today, I hope he would have put in *she* as well as *he*.

The *'clean hands'* seems to me to be the ritual part of it, but it doesn't go far enough. Pontius Pilate tried washing his hands of responsibility for Jesus but it isn't as easy as that. David added something altogether more demanding - *'and a pure heart'*. Throughout his life David had a problem living up to it, and so do we.

We make sporadic efforts but they don't last. Somehow we lose the motivation. It's significant that when we describe a lack of commitment we say 'my heart's not in it'. Someone said, 'Guilt isn't so much about what we do as about what we are'. It's about what goes on inside, something that Samuel emphasises in v. 7 when he reminds them that God looks deeper than we do, gets to the root within us and sees the motives for what we do.

It's the underlying bias that's important. Clean hands is one thing; the pure heart - the resolve to live up to the standards we know are right - is another. But that's what counts. The great thing is that God encourages us to keep on trying however many times we lose our way.

The outward bit's all right, Lord.
I can cope with that.
Clean hands.
As long as you don't probe too deep.
I can impress the casual onlooker.
I've learnt the words
and in all ordinary circumstances
I can strike the attitude
that fits the situation.
The words are there,
although they're just a thin veneer
that hides the underlying weaknesses.
Scratch the surface
and you'll find
a very different picture underneath.

It's not that I don't try.
I do.
But when the pressure comes,
my resolution sickens and grows weak
and, struggle as I may,
the inner tensions rise again.
The pure heart that I strive for
seems in almost constant need
of life support.
A daily case for intensive care
before it reaches terminal decline.

Lord, help me in the fight
that still goes on inside.
And when your hill seems steeper
than I can manage
and I stand gasping, near exhaustion,
give me the strength to start again.
However many times I slip,
take hold
and set me back on to my feet.
Return me to the path
and tell me yet again
I climb the hill with you.

But the Lord said to Samuel, 'Do not consider his appearance or his height, for I have rejected him. The Lord does not look at the things man looks at. Man looks at the outward appearance, but the Lord looks at the heart.'   1 Samuel 16:7

I wonder whether we value motive as much as we should. 'It's results that count,' we say. And certainly the world we live in concentrates on achievement. To be successful is all, to make money, to rise to the top job, to be the person with real influence. And if we don't make the grade, we're thought less of.

The other side of the coin is when we say, 'He meant well.' It usually has an underlying if unacknowledged implication of failure, and is used as a charitable excuse before we turn away. Meaning well doesn't seem to be enough.

Taking motives into account isn't easy. For one thing they can't be seen. They're in those hidden pigeonholes of personality that are hard to open. For another, human motives are often mixed, and our actions come from a jumble of selfish and unselfish attitudes. And if we can't know what's going on in anyone's mind then we need to give them the benefit of the doubt.

But surely what we intend is as important as what we achieve. We can't all reach the heights, but we can be sincere in what we try to do and be given some credit for it. David achieved a lot in his lifetime but a great deal of it was built on the backs of thousands of unknown people who just got on with the smaller things which supported and strengthened what he was led to do.

Samuel needed reminding to look deeper than the outward appearance, however attractive that might seem. And even though David is described later in megastar fashion, that's not why he was chosen. Honest, humble service ought to be valued as the great achievement it is and honoured more.

Even Samuel got it wrong, Lord,
sometimes,
so I'm in good company.
I think.

So eager for your work,
enthusiasm clouding judgement,
he grabbed the first conclusion
that looked him in the face.
Content with what he saw,
the easy answer,
the problem solved,
wrapped up and neatly put away.
Till you stepped in
and told him to dig deeper,
think things through
and wait for you.

Same thing with me.
The instant judgement made -
quicker than coffee in a mug
and just as comforting -
but usually wrong.
Lord, hold me back
until I've time to take a breath.
Time, if I'm pushed,
to pray,
although I don't do that
as often as I might,
and when I do
it's often as a last resort.
Time to look at things and people
with the eye of love,
your eye,
and leave the rest where it belongs.
With you.

'There is still the youngest,' Jesse answered, 'but he is tending the sheep.'
1 Samuel 16:11

J esse didn't even name his youngest son to Samuel. He was just the shepherd boy out on the hillside, too insignificant to be called to meet the prophet, and the sheep too valuable to be left.

Perhaps that was the way David was treated within the large extended family he was part of. There were eight brothers altogether. We're not told how many sisters, they seem to rate even lower than a younger brother during the patriarchal days in which this story was written down. And with the wives and babies of the older brothers, life must have been pretty crowded.

'Oh, you wouldn't want to see him,' Jesse tells Samuel. Jumping to conclusions can be dangerous and so can second-guessing other people's thoughts. How often I've heard someone say, 'Don't ask her, she wouldn't want to do that', without giving her the chance to speak for herself. Often people in that position do say 'no' because they sense that the enquiry is half-hearted anyway. Allow people the dignity of making up their own minds.

It's part of the respect we need to give to other people, and respect should have no sliding scale depending on age or status. And assessing status is a value judgement that takes us into very tricky territory. Jesus turned these judgements upside-down when he invited a child into the disciples' company.

I wonder if Samuel's heart jumped at Jesse's words. Did he see any significance in David being out tending the sheep? Kings in those days were often described as shepherds of their people. Certainly he wanted David brought quickly. And when David stood before Samuel, the encounter was enough to convince him that David was the one God wanted.

Lord, I'm thankful
that you've never put me down,
made me feel bad or worthless.

I've felt those things
more often than I care to count,
and sometimes deeply.
But when I think about it,
I see the hand of my own guilt at work,
my hand, not yours
My own creation,
a little monster brought to life,
perversely valued, running wild.
Keeping me distanced
from the love you offer.
You love me, not for any great achievement -
I am no David, Lord, nor even Samuel -
but for myself.
And not for what I might become
but as I am, right now.
It liberates me, Lord,
gives me the freedom
that I need to be myself.

I wish I had the grace
to see the world that way.
It's all so easy
putting people into pigeonholes
to sort and label,
young, old, or just plain awkward.
It leaves me feeling comfortable
to know where people stand,
and just a bit superior - nice feeling that -
although it never seems to last.

But that's not how you do it, is it, Lord?
Thank God, thank you for that.
For reasons I can't grasp you value me
and ask that maybe
I might do the same for others.
Show them the honour and respect
and, dare I say it, love
that takes them as they are.
Gives them the space to grow,
makes room for them in love
as you've made room for me.

So Samuel took the horn of oil and anointed him in the presence of his brothers, and from that day on the Spirit of the Lord came upon David in power. 1 Samuel 16:13

It's hard to imagine David's feelings as Samuel anointed him, but it's worth the effort. The youngest son, left out of the ceremonies, was now brought hot and sweating from the sheep on the hillside and swept before the prophet. During the time taken for a quick bath and a change of clothes, David's apprehension and excitement must have grown and reached its highest pitch as he stood facing Samuel.

David was highly intelligent, with a poet's sensitivity to the world around him. He was a skilled musician too and must have wanted more from life than caring for his father's sheep. Walking with them, lying in the shade of a tree, he must have had his teenage dreams. I remember my teenage dreams, although there are some I'd rather forget!

As he practised with his sling maybe David dreamed of becoming a warrior like his older brothers, and being a better one too. As he stood up and brushed the grass stalks from his homespun robe, did he dream of being wealthy, of having fine clothes and employing other people to watch the sheep? And with all those hormones rushing around his arteries any boy would dream of love. Why should David be an exception?

Then he was knocked sideways. Samuel's words brought utter surprise, created turmoil in his mind. This couldn't be true. Never in all his dreams had he thought to be king, yet the solemn anointing had to be taken seriously and would change his life radically.

The story moves me forward more than a thousand years to think again of Mary's feelings after the shepherds had visited her in the cave where Jesus had been born. '*But Mary treasured up all these things and pondered them in her heart.*' (Luke 2:19).

Each of them had to face a challenge that would change their lives completely. 'Why me?' they each must have asked. The working of God's spirit is as great a mystery for us today as it was for them. David couldn't get his mind around it, couldn't begin to understand, and found it hard even to believe that God had a purpose for his life. He just had to hold on to it and wait. And wait. That's hard.

Not in his wildest thoughts
could David have imagined
where you would lead him, Lord.
He had his dreams
of how he'd like to lead his life,
I'm sure of that.
Yearnings for better things,
hopes for a better world.
But dreams are delicate
and quickly bruised
on the sharp corners of reality.
Vulnerable to all the pressures of the day.
Easier to turn to disillusion
and think that dreams don't matter.
Images of adolescence,
innocence to be discarded.

Save me from that.
There's still a place for dreams.
Bright visions of a finer world
where love and mercy reign
and justice is the bottom line
of all our living.
Help me to hold my dreams secure.
To value them as treasure to be used,
not locked away like jewels in a box,
their iridescent beauty
wasted in the dark.

Help me to live my dreams.
To grasp the mystery with joy,
knowing that dreams
and what I call reality
all come from you.
That both are part and parcel
of my life with you.
Your spirit sowing dreams of what could be
and in their germination
enticing me to strive a little more,
to bridge the gap,
bring both together,
dream and reality in you.
Fulfilled.

So Samuel . . . anointed him in the presence of his brothers . . .
1 Samuel 16:13

There's no indication of how his brothers reacted to David's anointing. By the time the events in the next chapter took place we read of their anger towards David and assume their jealousy, but at the moment Samuel chose him their attitude is left without comment.

One can try to imagine it. Certainly they felt a similar surprise to David's, and a growing incredulity. This, their younger brother, the one who was sent out day after day to watch the sheep, to be king? They were older - the brothers not the sheep - stronger, more experienced. Already three of them were soldiers in Saul's army. David could never step into King Saul's shoes, command men, fight Philistines. Or so they thought.

Little did they know. It's often difficult to spot people's potential. I remember the head of a UK recording company admitting ruefully that when the Beatles came to him at the start of their careers he'd turned them down and said they'd never make it. Occasionally someone very bright pops up and you say to yourself, 'She'll go far', but usually identifying people's faults is a lot easier than identifying their possibilities.

In this case God made up Samuel's mind for him. St. Paul's words remind us that God chooses whom he wants and his judgement doesn't always coincide with ours.

'. . . *think of what you were when you were called. Not many of you were wise by human standards; not many were influential; not many were of noble birth. But God chose the foolish things of the world to shame the wise; God chose the weak things of the world to shame the strong. He chose the lowly things . . .*' (1 Corinthians 1:26 - 28).

And David must have seemed to his brothers to fit that description. But God knew what he was doing.

The way the Bible concentrates on essentials and often ignores the rest can be a bit frustrating. Even the reactions of David's father aren't mentioned, and there's no reference anywhere to his mother. We're not even given her name.

She wouldn't have been included in the ceremonies around the sacrifice. We can only guess at the mixture of pride and apprehension as she was told the details later of what was predicted for her youngest son. Her identity is submerged, another of those described by Paul's words, although her influence in forming David's character must have been vital, as any mother's is. She can't be identified but she isn't forgotten. Not by me anyway.

Not always easy, Lord,
to understand your mind,
to know the way you're thinking
and why things happen as they do.
Perhaps I shouldn't even try
but blind acceptance isn't in my nature,
however hard I struggle to conform.
The questions come unbidden,
uninvited guests who stretch their welcome,
stay too long for comfort,
and leave their cups unwashed.
But after all
my mind's your gift to me.
I'm only trying to use it.

The trouble is I'm often led
to seize the negative.
To see the seeming faults in what you do,
the weaknesses in those you call.
Forgive the arrogance
that makes me criticise so easily,
the ignorance that tempts me
into thinking that I know it all.
Sometimes I sense your smile,
an eyebrow raised in gentle ridicule
at all my posturing.

'Not many wise ...'
Yes, Lord, I know.
And in my better moments -
although they're not as many as I'd like -
I recognise
I'm just as weak and foolish
as I judge the rest to be,
and realise that strength and wisdom
are for you and you alone.

Lord, lead me deeper into understanding,
that I may look at others
through your eyes of love.
And if I can't see much in them that's promising,
help me at least to grant another chance,
a charitable benefit of doubt,
just as you do to me.

Part Two

Facing Reality

David and Goliath

Readings : 1 Samuel 17:16 - 24

For forty days the Philistine came forward every morning and evening and took his stand.

Now Jesse said to his son David, 'Take this ephah of roasted grain and these ten loaves of bread for your brothers and hurry to their camp. Take along these ten cheeses to the commander of their unit. See how your brothers are and bring back some assurance from them. They are with Saul and all the men of Israel in the valley of Elah, fighting against the Philistines.'

Early in the morning David left the flock with a shepherd, loaded up and set out, as Jesse had directed. He reached the camp as the army was going out to its battle positions, shouting the war cry. Israel and the Philistines were drawing up their lines facing each other. David left his things with the keeper of supplies, ran to the battle lines and greeted his brothers. As he was talking with them, Goliath, the Philistine champion from Gath, stepped out from his lines and shouted his usual defiance, and David heard it. When the Israelites saw the man, they ran from him in great fear.

1 Samuel 17:28 - 40

When Eliab, David's oldest brother, heard him speaking with the men, he burned with anger at him and asked, 'Why have you come down here? And with whom did you leave those few sheep in the desert? I know how conceited you are and how wicked your heart is; you came down only to watch the battle.'

'Now what have I done?' said David. 'Can't I even speak?' He then turned away to someone else and brought up the same matter, and the men answered him as before. What David said was overheard and reported to Saul, and Saul sent for him.

David said to Saul, 'Let no one lose heart on account of this Philistine; your servant will go and fight him.'

Saul replied, 'You are not able to go out against this Philistine and fight him; you are only a boy, and he has been a fighting man from his youth.'

But David said to Saul, 'Your servant has been keeping his father's sheep. When a lion or a bear came and carried off a sheep from the flock, I went after it, struck it and rescued the sheep from its mouth. When it turned on me, I seized it by its hair, struck it and killed it . . . The Lord who delivered me from the paw of the lion and the paw of the bear will deliver me from the hand of this Philistine.'

Saul said to David, 'Go, and the Lord be with you.' '

Then Saul dressed David in his own tunic. He put a coat of armour on him and a bronze helmet on his head. David fastened on his sword over the tunic and tried walking around, because he was not used to them.

'I cannot go in these,' he said to Saul, 'because I am not used to them.' So he took them off. Then he took his staff in his hand, chose five smooth stones from the stream, put them in the pouch of his shepherd's bag and, with his sling in his hand, approached the Philistine.

1 Samuel 17:48 - 50

As the Philistine moved closer to attack him, David ran quickly towards the battle line to meet him. Reaching into his bag and taking out a stone, he slung it and struck the Philistine on the forehead. The stone sank into his forehead, and he fell face down on the ground.

So David triumphed over the Philistine with a sling and a stone; without a sword in his hand he struck down the Philistine and killed him.

Imagine

Imagine the scene. Crowds of men are scattered over the hillside. Many still sit around the cooking fires, polishing their weapons, restringing and testing their bows. Some move around, finding friends they'll stand with in battle. Then the horns blow and people begin to move forward into rough lines, shouting their war cries.

Down the hill, beyond the forward lookouts, lies the valley with a shallow stream twisting and turning along its rocky bed. It marks the boundary. Then the ground slopes up again towards the Philistines' camp. In the distance they appear small, just a dark moving mass as they too get into formation. Their noise is covered by that of the Israelites, except for one voice, loud and rough, coming from the valley. Goliath is shouting. His language isn't understood by everyone but the aggression is quite clear.

King Saul stands on the upper slopes watching. This impasse has been going on for days and he's worried. So are his commanders. His army won't stay with him for long, their food has to be brought in from a distance, most of them are farmers and they have families to think about. Soon they'll begin to leave, slipping away quietly in the night. Saul needs a solution.

Someone tells him about David. Saul sends for him. Perhaps he recognises David as the young musician at court; maybe he's just grasping at straws, anything that might break the deadlock.

Take some time to imagine yourself into the feelings of three people: Saul, one of his commanders, and then David.

Saul is on edge. This may be just a large skirmish but if he loses it the Philistines could move on to attack Hebron. He's unsure. There have been several proposals for action, all faulty, but this confrontation must be ended. David volunteers to fight. He may be untried but he's an impressive young man. Saul feels some inner compulsion, a conviction he can't identify. Maybe the unexpectedness will give David an advantage. Saul doesn't know why, it seems risky, but before he knows what he's done, he's committed himself.

As a commander you're startled. After all the long and heated arguments in Saul's tent about tactics, here's the king making a key decision on the spur of the moment with no thought, no consultation. You're appalled. It's a colossal gamble. Goliath is a veteran, strong and aggressive. And who is this boy? You remember him vaguely as an occasional court musician. What's he going to do now. Hit Goliath with his harp? It's impossible.

How does David feel? He has an outward show of confidence, but his mouth's dry, his stomach churning as he realises that the king has agreed. Does he begin

The Dead Seas, towards Moab

to wish desperately he hadn't put himself in this position? Few people go into battle without fear. David's imagination races as he pictures himself down in the valley. What will he do when Goliath moves towards him? Bears attacking his sheep are one thing, but he's never killed a man. Will he have the strength and courage to go through with it? Will he even get a chance to strike? He takes several deep breaths, tries to control his thoughts, and reaches out to the God he's felt so close to on the quiet hillsides of Bethlehem. '*Are you still there? Can you help me now?*' he asks.

Now Jesse said to his son David, 'Take this ephah of roasted grain and these ten loaves of bread for your brothers and hurry to the camp.' 1 Samuel 17:17

We're given two accounts of how David progressed to the king's court. One through his music, being recruited to play his lyre to soothe the king (1 Samuel 16:18 - 23). The other was through his killing of Goliath. Both accounts can be reconciled.

David's job as musician gave him a place on the fringes of court life. Being part-time he was able to commute between home and court. This explains how he could be at home and able to take the food to his brothers before the battle. After Goliath's death David was recognised more clearly and *'From that day Saul kept David with him and did not let him return to his father's house.'* (1 Samuel 18:2). From then he had a full-time job.

Life's full of ups and downs. Whenever an experience takes us up to the heights we always seem to come down the other side into the depths. Maybe that means we're just getting back to normal which, by contrast with the high, seems low. If you see what I mean.

David couldn't have found it easy living with the promises that Samuel's anointing had brought. Promises that made David different, that filled his mind with questions about how and when he'd be king. Questions too about why he'd been chosen, and in the quiet moments waves of doubt must have begun to erode his confidence in God's purposes. There were certainly times when he felt isolated as family relationships changed. Change can create friction. It couldn't have been easy for any of them. When one family member's circumstances change, everyone has to adjust. It's no use expecting the one who's changed to go back to being what he was before. Change brings uncertainty.

His father brought David back to earth by asking him to take the bread and cheese to his brothers. What's more ordinary than bread and cheese? David had to get on with life and he did it with a rare humility.

The heights of spiritual experience don't give us permission to opt out of commonplace everyday responsibilities. I hope we accept them gladly and with a new awareness of God's presence and strength. Most of us are not called to be kings but to live faithfully where we are, knowing that God is with us in the workaday world.

David would need that awareness in the years ahead. Waiting for God's time is one of the most difficult lessons to learn and one of the hardest to accept. We want things to happen now. God often seems to have other plans.

In the rare moments, Lord,
of quiet -
which drop like little miracles
into the agitated waters of my life -
I feel you close to me.
I float in you,
enveloped and at peace.

But in the rush of life
the wave-beats drown your voice
and I am left alone,
or so it seems.
The contact's swamped,
the certainties eroded,
and questions,
how and why and when,
all lurking in the shadows of my mind,
take form and threaten.

Waiting for you,
not knowing all the details of your plans,
takes all my courage
and what little strength I have.
One moment reassurance lifts me up,
the next I don't know where to go.
Lord, help me catch
the faintest glimmer of your presence,
and when I can't see even that
strengthen my faith,
the faith that knows that you are near,
even - especially -
when the tide's run out
and I am beached in doubt.

The sea's still there.
Maybe I'm looking
in the wrong direction.

'Now what have I done?' said David. 'Can't I even speak?'
1 Samuel 17:29

History is a bit unfair to the Philistines. Call anyone a Philistine today and we imply that they're uncultured, ignorant, even barbarian. Whenever there's a disagreement about art or music it's not long before the word's used to suggest that someone's insensitive and without finer feelings. In Saul's day the Philistines were actually more sophisticated and had a better developed society than the Israelites, including the secret of producing iron. It didn't make them less brutal as soldiers but the Israelites equalled them there.

David had walked the fifteen miles west from Bethlehem and joined the Israelite forces. Morale wasn't too good. Neither side was keen to begin the battle. To do that they would have had to go down the hillside into the valley and then attack up hill. That would've been a hard thing to do with the defenders in a much stronger position. It was a stalemate, except for Goliath's daily provocation.

David looked and listened. Perhaps he was naive, but with the eagerness and bluntness of youth he began to ask awkward questions. He made people uncomfortable. 'How can this man defy the armies of the living God?' he asked, reminding them that God was alive; not just a tribal memory but a living reality.

He got under the skin of those who heard him, particularly his brothers. All their irritation and jealousy erupted into anger. They called him conceited and wicked and tried to put him down by asking sarcastic questions about where he'd left the sheep. David responded as young people the world over respond in their struggle to be accepted as adults. 'Now what have I done? Can't I even speak?' All the hurt and frustration obvious in his reply.

Youth has a habit of asking awkward questions we'd rather not confront. Questions about society's values, our behaviour and assumptions. Questions so challenging that the easy response is annoyance - a polite euphemism for anger - and a 'You don't really understand . . .'. If there's one thing young people are good at it's smelling out hypocrisy. That's one reason why they're difficult to live with.

Another may be that they make me ask David's question of myself. Am I simply living with a memory of God or is he still a living reality for me? It's a question I'm not always ready to face.

Misunderstood.
I know the feeling, Lord.
Words taken in a way I never meant.
Wrenched out of context,
warped out of true -
deliberately or accidentally,
I don't know which -
with all my explanations shrugged aside.

The trouble is
I've done the same to others.
Taken a word or comment
far too personally.
Given it a meaning
that was never meant,
and in response hit out,
bruising the truth,
leaving the speaker
with a hurt he didn't need,
much less deserved.

Lord, help me hear your purposes
in others' words.
Graft onto me the sensitivity I need
and let it grow and blossom
into the wisdom that accepts
that just occasionally -
humility's blue moon! -
I may be wrong.
Help me to see there's just a chance
the words that make me feel uncomfortable
and, let's be honest, angry,
are true and just.
That questions asked
which point with compass accuracy
to some deficiency in me
may have their origin in you.
And as I face myself
with less pretence than usual,
help me to make the changes
that will shape me
just a little more
into the likeness of your son.

'I cannot go in these,' he said to Saul, 'because I am not used to them.' 1 Samuel 17:39

Saul attempted to dress David in his armour. The image that comes to mind is almost slapstick comedy with David nearly engulfed in a tunic and helmet far too big for him. Saul himself was a big man. Maybe not Goliath's size but we're told that Saul was '. . . *without equal among the Israelites - a head taller than any of the others.*' (1 Samuel 9:2).

The king's armour would have been too heavy and restricting. A tunic down to mid thigh and covered in overlapping bronze plates, a helmet slipping over David's eyes, a sword long enough for David to trip over as he tried to walk. And David the shepherd boy would hardly have been skilled in the use of the sword. I'd rather not visualise the looks on the commanders' faces as they watched the charade. Goliath might have died laughing but not otherwise.

'It's no good,' said David, 'it's not me.'

Saul was trying to make David into something different; recreate him in his own image. Trying to force David into a mould he wasn't suited for, turning him into a conventional warrior when something different was needed. David would have none of it.

But we do it all the time and have it done to us. 'This is the way a Christian should act,' we say or, 'You can't do that.' We try to dress people with our own expectations, from the best of motives but without respect for personality. We even submit to other people's rules ourselves. Its result is to restrict the joy and freedom Christ offers us. In the end, although it's meant to protect us, all it does is weigh us down and hold us back.

Letting people be themselves seems to be something we're not very good at. We find it easier to give them a set of rules. I remember years ago as a young Christian worker in India trying to live up to an image of what I ought to be and do which had been grafted onto me by other people. It wasn't comfortable and it didn't work because it was a pretence. Eventually I realised that the only way to be real was to be myself, and that was how God accepted me anyway. There was no need to be anyone else, no need to play a role or to be a hero, saint or martyr. I could shrug off all the ill-fitting clothing others had suggested I should wear and simply live as me for the one '*whose service is perfect freedom*', as the Book of Common Prayer puts it. It was such a relief.

Lord, the clothes that other people
want to make me wear
don't fit.
I've tried them on,
buttoned and zipped,
stood at the mirror of approval
and twirled in all directions.
I've tried so hard to wear them in,
get used to them,
and still it doesn't work.

And now I've given up.

Not easy, Lord,
to take them off.
And stepping out of them
has left me feeling naked.
Exposed.
It's taken all my courage
to face the occasions
when, in innocence,
if that's the word,
and if I've any left,
I thought you wanted me to be like that.
To fit the pattern
and pretend the pattern fitted me.
But lies are not for living
however good the cause may seem,
and now I've reached the point of knowing,
with your help,
that all that matters
is the honesty to be myself.
Not in rebellion
but in knowing that
whatever others think of me
the judgement that I value most
is yours.
And that's a judgement that I know
clothes me in love
and accepts me for myself.

So he took them off. 1 Samuel 17:39

It's not always easy taking off the armour we wear, because it's not always other people who insist that we wear it. There're times when we're only too happy to put on armour for our own protection.

We armour ourselves against other people. We put on a front of self-sufficiency because we don't want them to invade our space, don't want to be disturbed, and instead of welcoming others we shelter behind the barriers we erect. Sometimes we're scared of showing our real feelings because we might be laughed at or hurt or rejected. So we live a pretence, wearing our armour and hiding behind the roles we play, the masks we wear.

And we armour ourselves against ourselves. It takes courage to look at what we really are, and face it honestly and openly, because it isn't always very nice. We feel it's better to let it lie undisturbed, sleeping dogs and all that, but we can only expect God to help us deal with it when we open ourselves up and take the armour off.

That's another thing - we hide behind our armour from God. All that goodness and holiness, that all consuming love is more than we can cope with. We're frightened to get in too deeply, and struggle to shield ourselves from him.

Whatever the reason we have for wearing our armour, taking it off makes us vulnerable, but it also makes us free. When David took off Saul's armour he found he was better able to fight the battle ahead of him. He may have been unprotected but he wasn't defenceless. God was with him.

You're on the edge, Lord, of my world,
not in the centre as you should be.
I'd like you there with me,
but I'm not ready yet
to open up and let you in.
Your foot is in the door,
that's fine.
I feel I'm in control,
can open it, or close it
as I choose.
But more than that seems dangerous.
I build defences.
Stay close-bound
inside a hard defensive shell
of spurious security.
And lobster-like,
close carapaced within my fear,
wave warning claws
against your loving hands.

Not only you, Lord,
distanced by my doubt.
I hide from others too.
Show only what I think they want to see
and grudgingly at that.
Can't find the openness
to share the truth with them.

And when I change direction,
look inside,
it's me I'm hiding from as well.

Lord, keep on knocking,
and let the probing fingers of your love
open the door a little more.
There's just a chance,
one day,
I'll really let you in
and find the will
to show myself to you,
to them and even to myself
just as I am.
Accept the freedom that you give
to be myself
and build on it with you.

Then he took his staff in his hand, chose five smooth stones from the stream, put them in the pouch of his shepherd's bag and, with his sling in his hand, approached the Philistine.   1 Samuel 17:40

From the height of the hill where David stood looking down, I imagine Goliath didn't look so big. I remember a story of an African bushman on his first flight in an aeroplane. Looking down on the open grassland, he was told that the black dots below were elephants. 'No, they must be ants,' he replied, 'they're not big enough for elephants.'

Perspective does that sort of thing, but as David moved down into the valley appearances changed. Goliath seemed to get bigger and bigger. He loomed large, threatening, dwarfing everyone and everything.

David was living out an experience common to most of us. From the mountain top, when we're on a high, everything seems fine and manageable, but when we sink down to the depths of the valley, pressures mount. The further down we go the bigger the giants seem, the more threatening the dangers.

As faith is tried and doubts grow we create our own giants. Goliath was real enough to David, and so are some of the problems we face. But others are imaginary, born out of our insecurity, although the imaginary giants are still real to those who suffer them. They all have to be dealt with.

All the time I've been thinking about taking off our armour in order to become real people, another thought's been niggling away. What about the call to '*Put on the full armour of God . . .*'? (Ephesians 6:11). There's no contradiction. If you read a bit further the armour is described - the belt of truth, the breastplate of righteousness, the shield of faith. And it's only as we work with God to peel away the layers of self-deception and fear that stunt our growth that we can stand in his strength rather than our own.

I have my own Goliaths, Lord.
Problems and people
looming large,
their shadows
darkly cast across my path.
Some creep up quietly,
lying in wait to overwhelm.
Others stand high and threatening
and I'm afraid.

It wasn't always so.
Up on the mountain top with you
I felt secure.
Could conquer anything from there.
'Your strength sufficient ...' and all that -
I'm sure you know the quote.
But as I face reality
the problems seem to grow
like Alice in a worried Wonderland,
and confidence diminishes
the deeper I descend.
My weapons seem so small and weak
against the titans in the valley.

Strengthen my arm.
Help me dispel the self-created giants
in my mind,
imaginary ogres living on my fears.
And when the ones I face
are real,
remind me in the depths
that you are there,
offering an armour
I can wear in confidence.
And in a love that frees me
from anxiety
I can step out in faith.
And win.

As the Philistine moved closer to attack him, David ran quickly towards the battle line to meet him.   1 Samuel 17:48

There's a time for prayer and a time for action, although many would say that prayer is action - just a different sort, and one that keeps us closer to God's purposes

David moved down the hill and as he went I'm sure he was praying. Nothing flowery or profound, just a simple 'Lord help me' kind of prayer. The prayer we all pray instinctively whenever we have problems. I say instinctively because people with no articulate belief, no habit of regular worship or church going, pray it when trouble threatens. It suggests that religious experience is deeper and more widespread than we sometimes think and that we all share a feeling that there's more to life than we can see or measure.

Then came the time for action. David picked his stones from the stream bed, chose them with care. I used to view this part of the story with some scepticism, wondering how a strong man could be stunned, let alone killed, by a small stone. Then on one of many visits to the British Museum in London I saw on display a group of sling stones dug up in Israel by archaeologists. They were as big as cricket balls - the stones, not the archaeologists - and trials have shown that thrown by an expert a stone like these can travel at a hundred miles an hour. That makes the situation real.

As David stood up on the edge of the stream, hefting a stone in his hand, I see him looking at Goliath. I imagine his first thought - 'Gosh, he's big!' Then his second thought - 'He's so big I can't miss!' And he doesn't. The disadvantage turned to advantage by the young shepherd who's prepared to take risks for God.

Refusing to wear other people's armour, unwilling to play the role others expected of him, David was true to himself, strengthened by an unreasonable faith that God would help him. And using his own skills he triumphs.

Faith is unreasonable, it has to be. If we believed that only the possible was possible, there'd be no point to faith. And yet, unreasonable though it may seem, faith makes things happen again and again.

*Lord, give me the wisdom
to know just when to pray
and when to act.
It's all too easy to confuse
the two.*

*To curl up
piously to pray
and leave the work to others.
Tempting at times
to lean on you
to such a point
I never see the need
to make decisions,
and call the accidental happenings
around my life's periphery
your will.*

*And sometimes
in the heat of life,
its stress and busyness,
so much to do,
so little time to do it in,
the opposite is true.
And drowning in my diary
I lose touch with you.*

*Yet that's the time I need
the stabilising ballast of your presence
to hold me to my course,
steady
in any storm that comes.
It's hard to get the balance right,
to pray myself to action
and to hold you there,
a presence in the tempest
who will bring me through
to journey's end.*

Part Three

Broken Dreams

Open Spaces

Readings : 1 Samuel 18:1 - 9

After David had finished talking with Saul, Jonathan became one in spirit with David, and he loved him as himself. From that day Saul kept David with him and did not let him return to his father's house. And Jonathan made a covenant with David because he loved him as himself. Jonathan took off the robe he was wearing and gave it to David, along with his tunic, and even his sword, his bow and his belt.

Whatever Saul sent him to do, David did it so successfully that Saul gave him a high rank in the army. This pleased all the people, and Saul's officers as well.

When the men were returning home after David had killed the Philistine, the women came out from all the towns of Israel to meet King Saul with singing and dancing, with joyful songs and with tambourines and lutes. As they danced, they sang:

> 'Saul has slain his thousands, and David his tens of thousands.'

Saul was very angry; this refrain galled him. 'They have credited David with tens of thousands,' he thought, 'but me with only thousands. What more can he get but the kingdom?' And from that time on Saul kept a jealous eye on David . . .

1 Samuel 18:20 - 21

Now Saul's daughter Michal was in love with David, and when they told Saul about it, he was pleased. 'I will give her to him,' he thought, 'so that she may be a snare to him and so that the hand of the Philistines may be against him.'

1 Samuel 19:9 - 10

But an evil spirit from the Lord came upon Saul as he was sitting in his house with his spear in his hand. While David was playing the harp, Saul tried to pin him to the wall with his spear, but David eluded him as Saul drove the spear into the wall. That night David made good his escape.

Imagine

Things don't happen all at once. Sometimes the Bible compresses stories with little indication of the time-scale. We don't know whether these events took place over weeks or months, although months seems more likely.

Imagine David's feelings and thoughts over this next period. Everything is going well for him. His dreams are coming true. His friendship with Jonathan is very important to him, not simply because Jonathan is the crown prince but because a genuinely warm relationship is growing between them. How did David feel as Jonathan gave him valuable and significant gifts, his own robes, his own weapons? Feel the softness of the cloth. Tighten the leather belt around your waist and feel the weight and hardness of the sword.

David begins to feel more confident as his experience grows of commanding soldiers in battle. Michal, the king's daughter, has fallen in love with him. What more could he ask?

But slowly the atmosphere begins to change. A man with his sensitivity as a poet and musician is surely aware of this. Saul is less friendly, not so open or welcoming. David catches Saul staring at him from time to time. The relationship begins to cool. His opinion isn't asked for so often. He's accused and blamed for things he hasn't done. David is bewildered. 'What's got into him?' David wonders, 'What have I done?'

Then comes the crisis. David is playing his harp. Saul is restless, that's why David is playing, but the music doesn't soothe Saul any more. It's become an irritant. Saul stands up, agitated. He moves to the wall, takes down a javelin, balances it in his hand. 'Why has he done that?' David is alert, his muscles tense even while he continues to pluck the strings.

Then with a sudden lunge Saul throws the spear hard and fast. Remember Saul is a warrior too. But David moves quickly - he's learnt that in the desperate hand to hand fighting he's been in - and as his harp skids across the floor, the javelin narrowly misses and finishes quivering in the woodwork of the wall behind him. There's a shout of rage and anguish from Saul as he staggers to the door, leaving David's dreams, if not David himself, pinned to the wall.

Shadowed Valley

Jonathan took off the robe he was wearing and gave it to David, along with his tunic, and even his sword, his bow and his belt.   1 Samuel 18:4

Davids dreams seemed to be working out although there must have been times when he found it hard to believe that what was happening was real. He'd come a long way in a short time, from watching sheep on a Bethlehem hillside to living in the king's palace.

His clothes no longer smelled of sheep, there were no worn patches or grass stains on them any more. He was wearing clothes given to him by the king's son, Jonathan, along with the sword and the bow. This was a great honour and we don't hear of David's sling again.

Jonathan moved in and out of David's life as a true friend. At times he was torn by conflicting loyalties, supporting and defending David yet staying with his father, trying to mediate and finally dying with Saul.

The emphasis on clothes intrigues me. Earlier David had refused to wear Saul's armour, rejecting the attempt to put him into clothes that didn't fit him. Now though he accepts a rich robe and tunic from Jonathan. Why the change? I believe that the difference was that these were given as a sign of friendship, gifts offered in love. Jonathan appeared to attach no demands to them, made no unreasonable expectations. That's the way love works.

Love accepts us for what we are, makes no threatening demands for change, simply supports and encourages. Friendships flourish where there's acceptance and founder when we try to remould people. Jonathan accepted David unconditionally, the way God through Jesus accepts us.

That's not to say we stay the same throughout a relationship. Friendships develop and progress. The important thing about our relationship with God is that he welcomes us as we are but then encourages the relationship to deepen as we are ready for it. David came to learn that slowly, and sang about it later. *'You turned my wailing into dancing; you removed my sackcloth and clothed me with joy.'* (Psalm 30:11).

Love accepts.
Lord, I try to get my mind round that
but stretch it how I may
I can't embrace the world of meaning that it holds.
Your love accepts me as I am.
Not to transform me into someone else
or something different,
and not for anything I've done.
Nothing to do with who I am
but who you are.
It isn't always easy to take in.
And harder to accept.

And still I find myself at times
trying to earn your love.
Make myself worthy,
offer you some quid pro quo -
I'm sure you know the Latin, Lord,
a lot of people seem to think so anyway.
I find it hard to take love as a gift
unmerited,
no strings attached,
just offered out of friendship.

Friendship.
A word devalued in our currency,
its daily market rate
vulnerable to every speculation.
Too weak a word
for what you offer, Lord,
and yet it packages so much.
A Tardis room containing more
than ordinary dimensions can allow
of love and constancy
which overflow,
engulf my life and hold me close.
I thank you for it, Lord.
And for a chance
to lose the guilt
that says I'll never measure up
to what you want.
When all you want, in fact, is me.
Your love will do the rest.

And from that time on Saul kept a jealous eye on David.
1 Samuel 18:9

Saul should have been grateful both to God and David. His decision to allow David to fight Goliath had been the right one. The giant was dead, and the imminent threat of a Philistine attack checked. Now they were able to return to their people in triumph.

But the presence of David, the young attractive hero, was giving a new focus to the people's attention. Saul wasn't happy. We don't know at what point he heard of Samuel's prediction for David's future, but whether he knew it or not at this time Saul could accept no one taking any credit from him. He wanted it all.

The singing, dancing crowd of women must have been impressive. The enthusiasm and noise, the sheer excitement of their reception should have been enough for anyone, but their compliments rankled. *'David has slain his tens of thousands'*? The words weren't meant to be taken literally. This was poetry, the sort of exaggeration we hear in opera or pop song, depending on which we enjoy most. But Saul interpreted it too personally.

He was still king but his insecurity was fertile ground for the seeds of jealousy beginning to germinate and root deep within him. He took no joy in David's success, seeing everything in the most negative way he could. The bottle was always half-empty, never half-full.

That's the trouble with insecurity, it can't build, only destroy. Saul was in a hole and digging it deeper, his personality shrivelling as he began his unpredictable slide into paranoia. If only he could have paused, taken a deep breath and counted his blessings. He was king, his people safe, and he'd found a new young warrior who could make him stronger. Counting blessings is more productive than holding on to hurts.

Easy to say, Lord,
'Count your blessings'.
And on a good day,
when Spring is in the air,
horizon sunshine clear,
and everything's gone right,
my spirit wakes,
stretches its arms to joy.
It's easy then.
The alleluias tumble out of me so fast
my feet trip over them.

But come the day
when cold winds blow
and things go wrong,
relationships and circumstances
warp and dislocate,
they soon outweigh the good.
And in the winter of my discontent
- to steal a phrase -
there seems much less to count.
The balance changes
and the joy's subdued,
shadowed by cloud.
Have patience with me, Lord.
And blame ingratitude on indigestion.
Something I ate.

Help me repaint the landscape
of my life in light.
Mix me warm colours
to replace the dark.
Remind me gently,
gently, Lord - I feel a little fragile -
that all's not lost.
There's still a sun behind the clouds
and seen or unseen
your love remains
and that's a blessing
I can count on
all the time.

The next day an evil spirit from God came forcefully upon Saul.
1 Samuel 18:10

This part of the story leaves me with a problem. *'An evil spirit from God'*? It's described that way twice, in this verse and in chapter 19:9, so we can't just ignore it. But to be honest, I don't believe it, can't believe it.

God is good, the whole emphasis of the Bible tells us that. *'God is light; in him there is no darkness at all'* as John's first letter puts it. That's not simply talking about the level of illumination. Light stands for all that's holy and good and true. Darkness is the opposite and, while it may have been entering Saul's personality, I don't believe it came from God.

Think of the songs David sang. 'I trust in God's unfailing love for ever and ever . . . in your name I will hope, for your name is good.' (Psalm 52:8 - 9). There's another recorded in 2 Samuel 22:29, 'You are my lamp, O Lord; the Lord turns my darkness into light.' It comes again in Psalm 18:28, with the words changed slightly, 'You, O Lord, keep my lamp burning', encouraging us with the knowledge that it's a continuous process. Perhaps Saul's trouble was that he couldn't hold himself open to the oxygen of God's presence that would keep the flame alive. See how soon a candle snuffer quenches the flame.

In the time when this history of God's people was written down it was believed that God controlled everything directly. They assumed everything came from him - illness, calamity, famine. And the only way they could make sense of Saul's predicament was to put the responsibility onto God. From our perspective we'd put it differently, a perspective illuminated more brightly by the revelation in Jesus of a loving and compassionate God.

There's still a place for judgement but we bring that on ourselves by smothering the light and warmth his presence offers. Saul turned his back on the Lord. It's no use blaming God for what we bring on ourselves. The responsibility lies with us.

You take a lot of blame, Lord,
for things you haven't done.
Must try your patience,
or would do if it wasn't infinite.
Thank God, thank you
for that.

It's all so easy,
faced with tragedy
and all the lesser happenings in life
that we find hard to live with,
to point accusing fingers
and heap responsibility on you.
An act of God, we say
and turn away,
the puzzle solved,
no blame attached to us.
Content to think that you
could blight the beauty of creation -
your creation, Lord -
with pain.

Agony there is,
and was,
a garden full of it,
the seeds of suffering
sown by human failing,
not by you.
Your role to take the hurt
upon yourself
and through the alchemy of love
transmute it into hope
greater than gold
Your presence in the pain,
a promise of new life.
And though we turn away from you,
you wait at every corner
offering
in loving patience yet again
a chance of restoration.

The choice is mine.

. . . the Lord was with David but had left Saul.   1 Samuel 18:12

Some people will be better able than I am to imagine the black despair that was weighing Saul down, tearing his personality apart. The writer describes it as the Lord leaving Saul. That was the way it seemed, and the way it seems to people who suffer similarly today. 'God's turned his back on me. I'm alone.'

It's not so, I'm sure of that. God isn't in the business of rejection. There's nothing we can ever do to stop God loving us. His arms are always open, his door never shut, unless we shut it ourselves. That's what Saul had done, he'd begun to build walls that would keep God out of his life.

It's better understood if we go right back to the time when Samuel anointed David. Samuel's insight was that Saul had been rejected *as king* (1 Samuel 16:1). That's different from his being rejected as a human being. Going back a little further we find the reason. Saul had begun to ignore God's will and make decisions which weren't in keeping with his role as God's chosen king. He'd decided he could go it alone without help from God.

The initiative towards tragedy was Saul's, and God could only wait for Saul's turning back to him. There was no question of punishment either. God is merciful, not vindictive, gracious and not vengeful. There's a helpful definition of mercy and grace:-

'God's mercy lies in not giving us what we deserve. God's grace is giving us what we don't deserve.'

And I'm sure God grieved over Saul as he grieves over each one of us. Like Saul, we may deserve God's disfavour but his love is always available. With him there's always a second chance, but we have to take it.

Lord,
keep me from the pride
that says
I'm self-sufficient
and can live my life alone,
choose my own way
and manage without you.

It's tempting, Lord,
to break the fragile threads
that hold us close together.
They snap so easily,
but if they break
it's at my doing
never yours.
And even though I feel
an urge to stray,
stay near
and hold me close,
your love more prodigal
than I deserve.
Help me to see
that freedom is illusion
without you.
An insubstantial mirage
shimmering before me,
dancing me deeper
into a desert of self-will,
despair the only drink,
and where my hopes
are bleached to bone.

My freedom lies in you.
A lesson I must learn again.
Your arms embrace,
not to control but comfort.
You are the oasis that I seek,
to green my life,
renew its fruit.
And if I ever grieve you
in my inconstancy
then draw me back again.

While David was playing the harp, Saul tried to pin him to the wall with his spear, but David eluded him as Saul drove the spear into the wall. That night David made good his escape.   1 Samuel 19:9 - 10

Dreams do sometimes come true, but they're often qualified by the reality of everyday life. There isn't much room for Walter Mitty types who live in a world of fantasy.

David's dreams seemed to be coming true. He'd become part of the king's favoured circle and a recognised leader. The king's daughter Michal had fallen in love with him and they had married. The only problem was his father-in-law. We're not told anything about his mother-in-law so there are no cheap jokes there. Relationships weren't easy. The king's power was absolute in human terms and his word was law, even when it was unlawful.

Struggling to stay loyal, David used his music to comfort and reassure Saul but it didn't work. The crisis came. I hear the thoughts going through David's mind. It seemed strange that Saul would sit in the palace holding his spear. Why would he do that? Weapons had to be cleaned but surely servants would do it. To practise his technique? You don't do that indoors. It put David on edge.

Saul was in a dark mood, brooding, his mind in turmoil. All the feelings of jealousy, anger and alienation were welling up inside him, and in one awful moment of violence his spear pinned all David's dreams to the wall. So quickly done.

It's so easy to throw spears. The angry comments, the barbed remarks we make with no thought of consequences, the sarcasm that shatters confidence and hurts without consideration. It's not always easy to hold the words back. It may be important to let people know how we really feel when we've been hurt but there are better ways of doing it. We're more likely to get a helpful response when we do it with loving kindness as a weapon.

*Lord, I remember times
when I've been hurt.
Targeted and pinned down
by criticism.
Motives misunderstood,
often deliberately
or so it seemed,
and I've been left with wounds
that take too long to heal.
And then I find
it's hard to hold my tongue
and count to ten,
though often ten's not quite enough,
a hundred might be better.*

*And when the hurricane's blown out,
the words that hurt as I've been hurt
all spoken,
I see around my feet
the shredded remnants
of my resolutions to do better.*

*Then, Lord, forgive
and in your gentle way,
your voice not in the earthquake,
wind or fire,
point me once more
along your path.
Give me the grace,
so undeserved,
to put resentment
in its place.
Not buried deep
below the surface of my life
to sprout again unnoticed
when I least expect it,
but at your feet
where you and I
together
can recycle it as love.*

Part Four

The Waiting Game

Oasis at Noon

Readings : 1 Samuel 24:1 - 7

After Saul returned from pursuing the Philistines, he was told, 'David is in the Desert of En Gedi.' So Saul took three thousand chosen men from all Israel and set out to look for David and his men near the Crags of the Wild Goats.

He came to the sheep pens along the way; a cave was there, and Saul went in to relieve himself. David and his men were far back in the cave. The men said, 'This is the day the Lord spoke of when he said to you, "I will give your enemy into your hands for you to deal with as you wish." ' Then David crept up unnoticed and cut off a corner of Saul's robe.

Afterwards, David was conscience-stricken for having cut off a corner of his robe. He said to his men, 'The Lord forbid that I should do such a thing to my master, the Lord's anointed, or lift my hand against him; for he is the anointed of the Lord.' With these words David rebuked his men and did not allow them to attack Saul. And Saul left the cave and went his way.

1 Samuel 31:1 - 4

Now the Philistines fought against Israel; the Israelites fled before them, and many fell slain on Mount Gilboa. The Philistines pressed hard after Saul and his sons, and they killed his sons Jonathan, Abinadab and Malki-Shua. The fighting grew fierce around Saul, and when the archers overtook him, they wounded him critically.

Saul said to his armour-bearer, 'Draw your sword and run me through, or these uncircumcised fellows will come and run me through and abuse me.'

But the armour-bearer was terrified and would not do it; so Saul took his own sword and fell on it.

2 Samuel 1:17 - 19

David took up this lament concerning Saul and his son Jonathan, and ordered that the men of Judah be taught this lament of the bow:

> 'Your glory, O Israel, lies slain on your heights.
> How the mighty have fallen!'

2 Samuel 2:4

Then the men of Judah came to Hebron and there they anointed David king over the house of Judah.

Imagine

Take time to imagine David's feelings as a fugitive. The sudden shock as Saul threatens to kill him. The desolation that comes when he realises that he must abandon everything to save his life - family and friends, Jonathan, his position, even his wife. His world is shattered. Imagine the feeling of unreality, the disbelief, the denial that this could be happening.

Out in the Judean desert life is hard. High stark cliffs throw heavy shadows across jagged rocks. The cliffs are riddled with caves. There are deep valleys strewn with stones and straggling thorn bushes. The days are burning hot with a dry, desiccating heat; the nights cold and long. Here and there you find a small patch of green grass and a few palm trees. An oasis with a well, even a small struggling stream.

David has come to one at En Gedi. It's evening, the sky transformed from burning gold to gentle pink and grey. As the last light fades David and his men sprawl around a small fire in the mouth of the cave they've chosen to shelter them through the night. The air is suddenly chill as the sun dips below the horizon.

David takes his lyre and moves a little way up the hillside, past the lookout who watches for signs of pursuit. They rarely feel safe. David's feelings are as bleak as the ground he walks on. He sits against a rock and as the sky darkens he looks up at the first stars. He plucks a few notes on the harp and begins to sing softly.

> 'Deliver me from my enemies, O God; protect me from those who rise up against me.
> Deliver me from evildoers and save me from bloodthirsty men.'
> (Psalm 59:1 - 2).

It's a protest song, and David's anger spills out against his enemies, against his circumstances and, truth to tell, against God. But gradually his mood changes as he finds release from the tension and he reaches out in longing towards God. He can't always understand what's happening to him but he holds on to his faith even when God seems distant.

> 'O God, you are my God, earnestly I seek you;
> my soul thirsts for you, my body longs for you,
> in a dry and weary land where there is no water.'
> (Psalm 63:1).

It's only those who've travelled in the desert and know what real thirst feels like who can truly imagine David's longing.

Judean Desert

Deliver me from my enemies, O God; protect me from those who rise up against me. Psalm 59:1

There must have been times when David's only release came through his music. His life had changed dramatically. He'd fled from Saul into the dubious safety of the desert. His flight mirrored that of Moses centuries earlier running from Egypt's Pharaoh. Like Moses, David was living hand to mouth as a fugitive. Maybe his youthful life as a shepherd had been a kind of preparation but it was still as traumatic an experience as it had been for Moses.

It made David angry and it all spilled out in this psalm. Read the whole of it. It may be part of the Bible but it's not easy to read. There's an uncomfortable vindictiveness in some of the words. There's no doubting how he saw his persecutors and how he wanted them dealt with. He wanted them punished, wanted to gloat over them. He doesn't name them but he'd like to see them suffer as he had. It was very human, if not very edifying.

The reassurance for me is that David couldn't keep it up. Even in his angry attempts to get God to punish, David held on to a conviction that God is a loving God, even though he was trying to limit God's love to himself and withhold it from his enemies.

It also comforts me to realise that there is no psalm beginning 'There is no God.' However great David's sufferings and frustration became, he still held on to his conviction that God was there and was listening.

There's a place for anger, and not just righteous anger. Anger is there, deep down in all of us, and it has to be acknowledged and dealt with. I'm sure God can take with compassion the harshest words we can think of when our distress is real and deep. And even when our anger is directed at God, as I suspect David's was, it's important that we bring it out into the open before him. If we hold the anger down and pretend it's not there, we're living a lie. Going back to an earlier thought, we're wearing clothes that don't fit and it won't do us any good. God's love is unqualified, and far from punishing us for our anger he'll help us deal with it.

I'm only human, Lord, as David was,
although I can't compare myself
to him, and don't.
But I get angry too at times.
Frustration spilling out
when things go wrong.
When difficulties lie in wait
to bring me down.
Ambush my hopes
and leave my good intentions
bleeding on the ground.

And then, Lord, anger erupts.
A lava flow that threatens everything in sight.
An incandescence
surging up from deep inside,
releasing thoughts and feelings
I hardly knew existed
and wish I didn't now.
A violence
that batters down restraining walls
I've taken years to build.

I look around eager to identify
an easy enemy to blame.
A scapegoat I can heap my anguish on.
But when, nearly engulfed,
I call on you for help,
your voice comes through the storm.
Not always bringing peace
but bringing truth.
Offering an understanding that helps me light
the still dark corners of my life,
identify the untamed prisoner within,
who stands reluctant to release the bars
he grasps so tight
of self-inflicted prison.
Resisting to the last
the open door to life and freedom.

Lord, in your mercy deal with me
as once you did with David.
Cradle me in love
and bring me through the valley
to your peace.

After Saul returned from pursuing the Philistines, he was told, 'David is in the Desert of En Gedi.' 1 Samuel 24:1

There was little let up for David and his followers. From the time he fled from Saul they were almost constantly on the move, a band of guerrillas fighting to survive in the wilderness of the Judean desert. Occasionally there was respite. En Gedi was, and still is, a lovely oasis of green around a permanent fresh water supply on the western edge of the Dead Sea.

In David's time it was a farming town. The Song of Songs, which many believe was written by Solomon, David's son, refers to *'the vineyards of En Gedi'* (Song 1:14), a fertile and productive centre of crops and wine. A wonderful place for people who'd had a hard time in the desert. But David couldn't relax in the town. It was too dangerous. He and a small group of his men hid quietly in nearby caves.

They must have known a moment of panic thinking they were trapped as Saul came near, but the tables were turned as Saul entered the cave alone. He was in their power. All it needed was one quick thrust with his sword, the sword Jonathan had given David, but whatever pressures were put on him at that moment, he held back.

There's a time for action but there's also a time for reflection, and David takes it. It must have been tempting. Just one move, one decision, and his problems would've been solved. But that one action, tempting though it must have seemed, was just that - temptation.

The end didn't justify the means, and never does. It can seem so easy to make an immediate decision like that, but if it involves wrongdoing of any sort it can't be right. I don't think God has the word expedient in his vocabulary. Hard though it was, David chose to wait for God's timing.

A time for action
and a time to wait.
My problem, Lord,
is knowing which is which.
Not always easy to decide
when I should act
and when a situation
needs more thought.

Action is tempting.
The macho move
that could resolve
my inconvenience at a stroke
and show me strong and masterful
- the fantasy is nice, Lord,
even though it never seems
to work like that.
I hesitate,
and wonder if it's really strength -
weakness can wear a dubious authority -
or simply an impatience to be done.
An intolerance of things and people
I find hard to live with.
Love works by bringing opposites together
in love's time.
Sometimes it needs a miracle,
but love is more acceptable than hate
to build my life upon.
But in my quiet moments
sometimes I find
more questions than I've answers for.
And in the end I have to leave
my problems and uncertainties with you.
As David did.
Confident - I wish I were -
that all things shall be well at last.

Lord, grace me with your wisdom,
a little is enough for now,
and just a bit of understanding.
Help me to see each situation
with your eyes
and act, when action's needed,
with a sympathy
that can only come from you.

O God, you are my God, earnestly I seek you; my soul thirsts for you, my body longs for you, in a dry and weary land where there is no water . . . Psalm 63:1 - 4

These words come alive when you've travelled in the desert as I have in Ethiopia and Israel. David's words were heartfelt, arising out of real experience. There must have been many bleak moments for him during his years in the wilderness, times when he had to put on a mask of confidence to encourage his followers, even when he felt differently and God seemed far away.

Where was God? Why didn't he help? The questions must have tumbled through David's mind. Occasions when he had to hang on desperately to faith in the promises God had given him, and fight his doubts. The desert days may have been hot but it was cold midwinter in his heart.

You can read the words of this song in different ways. To me the revealing words are *seek*, *thirst*, *long*. This wasn't a song of satisfaction, but a cry for help. There's less need to seek or thirst or long for God if you can feel him near. David was reaching out for encouragement, but all he was finding was emptiness and silence. The desert was within, and in later verses of the psalm it seems that all David could do was to hold on to memories of days when he could feel God close.

At times we create a desert for ourselves, turning our backs deliberately on God, but at other times, in spite of all our longings, we hear no answer to our prayers. Our words just seem to disappear into nothing. God seems to have withdrawn. I don't know why. I wish I did. The Desert Fathers, the great saints, all experienced this seeming emptiness. Jesus knew it. Hanging on the cross he shouted a similar question, echoing the psalmist's words, *'My God, my God, why have you forsaken me?'* (Psalm 22:1).

That gives us a clue, because God hadn't abandoned Jesus. Far from it. God was there, suffering with him, and the purpose of the cross was realised. He's there with us too in the silence and the loneliness, and if we question it then we're only doing what Jesus did.

We don't know why it has to be this way. It would be so much easier if God simply jumped in at the instant we asked and made things perfect, but I'm not sure we'd grow into maturity that way. And whether we could bear the full glory of his presence is another question. Children need to move out of the protection of loving parents into what we call the real world - although I'm sure that love is part of the real world - and wise parents encourage them to do so. And as for making everything perfect, I think God's rather expecting us to have a go at that ourselves, with his help of course.

Lord, will I ever understand
those times
when all my cries bounce back
and echo through the empty silences
of life?
When you are far away,
or so it seems,
although I'm told you're always near?
When I reach out my hands
to grasp
and find I hold
nothing more substantial
than the air I breathe?

I scan my life's horizon
endlessly.
Eager to see that first small cloud
grow to a gift,
its promise insubstantial
on the first faint breeze.
Yearning to feel your presence
in the sweet glad smell of rain on wind
falling on the desert of my life.
And whether you come
in dew at dawn gently
or in raging storm
that lifts the roof
and floods each corner of my life,
I'll welcome it.

Meanwhile I wait for answers
but you seem content
to let me find my own,
although they never seem to satisfy.
Yet in the gap between us
the silence stirs,
alive with possibilities
I can't define
and somehow
making wordless promises
that fill the space
and change the stillness
to tranquillity.
I'll wait, Lord.

. . . in a dry and weary land where there is no water. Psalm 63:1

My mother used to try to temper my childish impatience with the words 'If it's worth having, it's worth waiting for.' Waiting is one of the most difficult things we're called on to do. We're impatient. We're an instant people, whether it's coffee or credit, and we want everything now. And to be impatient for spiritual experience is often seen as a virtue.

An American writer, Sue Monk Kidd, observes in her book *When the Heart Waits* that waiting is often thought of as a waste of time. But she says that's far from the truth. Waiting is a time of preparation. She looks at a cocoon spun by a caterpillar and realises that through the winter, when nothing seems to be happening, momentous changes are taking place within the cocoon, and that in time a butterfly will emerge. And to become a butterfly the cocoon can't be avoided.

We need to go through a cocoon stage in life if we are ever to develop further, and that stage in our journey can't be avoided or hurried. Waiting comes whether we wish it or not. Its length is not in our hands and it can happen even while we are apparently living and functioning normally. As it did with David.

David's waiting was in the desert, ours may be in the crowded city, but the experience is essentially the same. We too may become a *'dry and weary land where there is no water.'* And like David we may yearn for it to end, but that's not in our hands. How long we wait is God's decision and he won't be hurried. Rebelling doesn't help. The dry land needs the water but it has no power to make the rain come. That happens when God judges that the time is right.

All the dry land can do is wait. And if God seems far away we may need to hold on desperately to the memory of experiences of other days. The change will come. The cocoon will split eventually and the butterfly will spread its wings in beauty.

The important thing is that in our waiting we are turned in God's direction. Then the waiting will begin the metamorphosis that makes us into what he wants us to be.

Still waiting, Lord,
for that one touch
to open up my life to you.
I treasure moments
when I've felt at ease,
content to wait,
your presence gentle,
intimate and warm.
But now a cold wind blows,
shredding contentment.
Emptiness surrounds me,
draws me into darkness
and I feel alone.
I wait but nothing seems to happen
and time moves on without me.
Or so it seems.

Is there a chance
that you could reassure me
that the waiting's purposeful?
That waiting's never wasted
if it draws me nearer you.
That in the silence
and the dark
your will is working out
its possibilities?
And that the day will come -
soon, Lord, soon -
when shroud will split
and I will burst
the wall of my cocoon
and I'll emerge
into the fullness of your light.
Transformed.
And then
I shall unfurl my wings
and fly.
The chrysalis discarded,
metamorphosis complete,
the promise made reality.

How the mighty have fallen!   2 Samuel 1:19

Jonathan was dead, killed by the Philistines along with two of his brothers. Saul was wounded and surrounded. There seemed no way out and in despair Saul took his own life. A tragic end to a tragic career.

This final act was the climax to years of self-destruction. In all his agony it's fitting that no one else could be blamed for his death. And maybe too it's significant that nowhere in the description of Saul's end is there any suggestion that the hand of God was at work in it. Saul's decline was Saul's responsibility. No one else's. There lies the sadness.

The jealousy and hatred in his heart had blighted his life, corroding and poisoning his personality. Ill feelings, and these were more than that, always damage most the one who shelters them, whatever they may do to anyone else.

It's always sad to hear someone say, 'I'll never forgive him' for some real or imaginary hurt, or even, 'Yes, I can forgive him, but he'll have to make the first move.' It doesn't work that way. Forgiving is an essential part of our spiritual survival, not just our spiritual growth. Resentment sows the seeds of destruction and by holding on to it we kill ourselves by degrees. Strong words but true.

Whatever other people may do to me, whether accidentally or by design, there's little point in waiting for the other person to make a gesture of regret. The only way to break the vicious circle of anger is to do something myself for my own sake. In a sense one could almost say that the act of forgiving is selfish because it does me at least as much good as it does the other person. It releases my mind and allows my energies to be channelled into something more profitable.

Forgiving may seem like a little crucifixion but death on the cross leads to new life. And always did.

Lord, if I should ever seem
to hold resentment dear
and hoard the hurts
that life has brought,
remind me
that I'll hurt myself
more than I'll injure those
who bruise my toes.

And yet surrender can be hard.
Although the bitterness corrodes
and etches deep
into my being,
I still treasure it.
And like a miser
hide it secure and deep,
to take it out
occasionally
to count and gloat.
I'm rich,
if only in resentment.

Lord, break the chains
that hold me to my ills,
that multiply my rancour.
Give me the freedom
to forgive,
to open wide my life
and welcome
those I've fought against
so long and bitterly.
Help me to look
and see in them,
however faint,
your image.
And acknowledge
that you love them,
against the odds,
as you love me.
That way is life.

Then the men of Judah came to Hebron and there they anointed David king over the house of Judah. 2 Samuel 2:4

David had lived ten years in the wilderness, years of danger, struggle and deprivation. There must have been days when he was strongly tempted to give up, when God's promises seemed empty, and there was little satisfaction in carrying on the fight. Times when he wondered whether the promises had come from God in the first place or whether Samuel had made a big mistake. If David had given up, it wouldn't have seemed so much that he was turning his back on God but that God had apparently turned his back on him.

But after the tragedy and sadness of the deaths of Saul and Jonathan came the bitter-sweet moment which ended the years of waiting. David shrugged off the cocoon and emerged into the full light as king of Judah. It would take another seven and a half years for him to unite the whole of Israel and Judah, but this was the first big step.

As the leaders of Judah crowded round David to anoint him, his mind must have gone back to that private family occasion with Samuel which began it all - Samuel's quiet anointing of David and his sharing of God's promises.

The seeming emptiness of those desert years was now echoing with God's purposes and the realisation that he'd been in God's hands all the time. Not that God had willed the years of suffering - they were Saul's creation - but God had been working for good through them all.

Looking back on life we see things with a clarity we're never granted when we try to look into the future.

Lord, sometimes I'd like to see ahead
more clearly.
Dispel the mist
that swirls around the future
and makes my every move
a little problematical.
It would be nice, I feel,
if you could write
the next few steps of my itinerary
in greater detail.
I'd like a timetable reliably constructed,
its routes, departure and arrival times
defined with some precision.
I'm on the bus
and though the seats are reasonably comfortable
I'd like to see the way
more clearly than I do.

But when I think it through -
and that's an effort I don't always make -
I reckon that the reason
that my journey's not defined
is because you give me freedom
to choose the route I take.
Trusting me more, perhaps, than I trust you.
Your hope and expectation
that I'll step out
armed in the confidence
I've found from looking back
and seeing
that in good times and in bad
your presence gave me strength
and comfort.
I don't know what's to come
but that no longer matters
quite so much
as knowing that
whatever it may be
you'll be there
on the road with me.

Part Five

Final Movement

Oasis at En Gedi

Readings : 2 Samuel 11:1 - 5

In the spring, at the time when kings go off to war, David sent Joab out with the king's men and the whole Israelite army. They destroyed the Ammonites and besieged Rabbah. But David remained in Jerusalem.

One evening David got up from his bed and walked around on the roof of the palace. From the roof he saw a woman bathing. The woman was very beautiful, and David sent someone to find out about her. The man said, 'Isn't this Bathsheba, the daughter of Eliam and the wife of Uriah the Hittite?' Then David sent messengers to get her. She came to him, and he slept with her . . . Then she went back home. The woman conceived and sent word to David, saying, 'I am pregnant.'

2 Samuel 11:14 - 17

In the morning David wrote a letter to Joab and sent it with Uriah. In it he wrote, 'Put Uriah in the front line where the fighting is fiercest. Then withdraw from him so that he will be struck down and die.' So while Joab had the city under siege, he put Uriah at a place where he knew the strongest defenders were. When the men of the city came out and fought against Joab, some of the men in David's army fell; moreover, Uriah the Hittite died.

2 Samuel 12:1 - 7

The Lord sent Nathan to David. When he came to him, he said, 'There were two men in a certain town, one rich and the other poor. The rich man had a very large number of sheep and cattle, but the poor man had nothing except one little ewe lamb that he had bought. He raised it, and it grew up with him and his children. It shared his food, drank from his cup and even slept in his arms. It was like a daughter to him.

'Now a traveller came to the rich man, but the rich man refrained from taking one of his own sheep or cattle to prepare a meal for the traveller who had come to him. Instead, he took the ewe lamb that belonged to the poor man and prepared it for the one who had come to him.'

David burned with anger against the man and said to Nathan, 'As surely as the Lord lives, the man who did this deserves to die! He must pay for that lamb four times over, because he did such a thing and had no pity.'

Then Nathan said to David, 'You are the man!'

Oasis

2 Samuel 12:13 - 14

Then David said to Nathan, 'I have sinned against the Lord.' Nathan replied, 'The Lord has taken away your sin. You are not going to die. But because by doing this you have made the enemies of the Lord show utter contempt, the son born to you will die.'

Imagine

David is king. He has a firm hold on his people. He no longer leads his troops personally but sends them out under trusted generals. The winter snow and the early rains have given way to sunshine. The crops have been sown and there's a feeling of expectation in the air.

It's evening. It's been a warm day and now the sun is beginning to set over the western edge of the city. Jerusalem - *the city of peace* - seems peaceful, even though out to the east over the River Jordan David's troops are confronting their enemies.

It's a lovely time of day. The light is softening, its midday glare gone, the sky gentling into pale blues and pinks. All over the city cooking fires are being lit, spreading a soft blue blanket of smoke just above the roofs of the single-storied houses. The city is waking up, stretching itself after the afternoon siesta, the shops opening up again for evening trade. Apart from the shopkeepers people are beginning to relax, the day's work coming to an end. Little groups of men meet on street corners, coalesce and drift apart.

This is the time when personal defences are down and tiredness loosens the awareness. David is watching the sunset, enjoying the view, thinking with some satisfaction, 'All this is mine.' The city, its people, the surrounding land. It's been a long hard road, but now he can take a quiet satisfaction in what he's achieved. He enjoys the feeling of success, the sense of power as he clenches then relaxes his hands.

Jerusalem is a small city crowded on a hill, its buildings jostling for space. From where David is standing he sees a jumble of flat rooftops. He looks down on them and watches the life around him. There's grain on some, stored from the last harvest, fuel stacked on others. There are beds and sleeping mats laid out, and a few children playing a game. Then another movement catches his eye. He looks down and sees a woman bathing. He looks away, then looks again. She is beautiful. David is human, male, his pulses quicken.

He turns away, trying to control his feelings. But he can't resist another look. He turns back and is lost. After all he is king. He thinks he deserves some reward for the hard years of struggle, the responsibilities that pile on him each day. And . . . well, he's only doing what so many do . . .

Market at Hebron

The woman was very beautiful, and David sent someone to find out about her. 2 Samuel 11:2 - 3

David began well as king. He *'reigned over all Israel, doing what was just and right for all his people.'* (2 Samuel 8:15). Then comes this incident which takes my breath away. So far in this saga David had been the hero, the wronged and persecuted man chosen by God to lead his people. He'd held fast to faith through times of great difficulty and deprivation, sometimes easily, sometimes with a desperation we can only imagine. Suddenly, in the days of success, David made a wrong choice. And it wasn't just a small mistake.

Wouldn't it have been better if the Bible had glossed over this relationship? It couldn't have been ignored entirely because later David and Bathsheba had another son, Solomon, but it could have been played down, sanitised. It might have been more comforting for later generations to see David as the perfect man of God, but the Bible's too honest for that.

And in the end, letting us see this less attractive side of David's character makes him more human. Like most other people, famous or not, he's a wounded personality blown about by his own emotions and in need of the grace and healing that only God can give. There's encouragement in that, reminding us that God works through imperfect, vulnerable human beings with all their failings. That's just as well; if he only worked through perfect people he wouldn't get much done because there aren't many of them around.

But how did this happen? This was the same David who'd faced Goliath, confident in God's strength; the same David who'd held on to faith through all his years in the desert. Perhaps in the increasing busyness of life, through the growing responsibilities of leading his people, David found less and less time for God. His faith was put into a smaller and smaller compartment of his life and became something 'I'll get back to when I have time'.

The longer this separation went on the easier it became to make the division more complete.

And from being central to life, faith becomes at best something for Sunday morning - or in David's case for the Sabbath - but irrelevant to 'real' life. David shut the door on God and felt free to act as he wished with no thought of the consequences, either to him or to anyone else.

I must admit, Lord,
that I find it satisfying
to see the great and good and mighty
bite the dust.
To see them vulnerable and weak
and plainly in the wrong.
And if I never rise
to stand on pedestals with them
at least it's possible
to pull them down to where I am.

And yet I feel a sadness too at David's plight.
That he should come to this.
Your man, so full of promise.
The one you chose and helped
and guided over all the years.
But now, his conscience callused over,
nerve endings dulled,
insensitive to all the pain
he gave to others,
the hurt done to himself,
he takes what isn't his.

A lesson there for all of us to learn.
(I put it in the plural, Lord,
so that the accusation
doesn't get too personal
and I can keep a modicum of comfort.)
The message is quite clear.
Temptation comes to all.
Sometimes full frontal
- please forgive the phrase -
more often silent and invisible in its subtlety,
creeping unrecognised into our lives.
My life. (On second thought
I'd better put it in the singular again,
the plural is too tempting
and let's me off the hook too easily.)
And maybe just because
I've never shared a bed
with other people's wives,
the pride that says that is itself a sin.
Lord, keep me from quick judgement
of other people's pain.

'Put Uriah in the front line where the fighting is fiercest.'
2 Samuel 11:15

With God firmly locked out of his life David sank deeper into trouble. His sensitivity as a poet and musician should have helped him imagine the pain and desolation his behaviour could bring to everyone involved. During David's time as a fugitive, Saul had given David's wife to another man. Had he forgotten the hurt he'd felt then? But David's rise to power had overlaid those feelings. He now had the power to do what he wished and that was all that mattered.

Bathsheba was pregnant. Unsuccessful in deceiving Uriah into sleeping with his wife so that he would believe the baby was his, David moved from adultery, through deception, to murder. Somehow he was able to justify it all to himself. After all it wouldn't be his hand that killed Uriah, so it wouldn't be his fault. And maybe David said to himself, 'Well, God can protect Uriah if he wants too.'

'Power corrupts,' says the wise man and we all agree, but in agreeing we look at other people rather than ourselves. We apply it to politicians and newspaper editors, and fat cats in industry, but it comes much nearer home than that.

We all hold power of some sort, and we all misuse it. There's power within the family; the unconscious manipulation of feelings. The influence of parents over children for good or bad. The mood swings to get one's own way, the quarrels or the silences when words can't persuade. And children too quickly learn ways of getting what they want.

There are, God forgive us, similar struggles within our church congregations, sometimes blatant, more often exercised in hidden ways, and often in the name of God. Even powerlessness can become an instrument to manipulate opinion and decision-making, and become power in its turn.

We're quick to justify it to ourselves at least. We use our power 'for the good of everyone'. Or so we say, and often with a shallow and bogus sincerity that insulates us from the truth. Yet, however much we turn our backs on God, however hard we lean on the door to keep him out of those dark and hidden corners, he's there waiting patiently. He may seem threatening at times, I'm sure David must have felt that, but he's waiting to restore, not condemn.

His presence isn't always gentle. He can create unease, put quiet questions into our minds, leave us uncomfortable and disturbed, but only to bring us back to himself. However much we may deny it, our hearts are restless until they find their rest in God, as Saint Augustine found.

One thing leads to another, Lord.
It's all so easy
having taken one small hesitant step
to take the next.
To tell myself
it doesn't really matter.
I'm not a murderer,
my sins are small
compared to some.
And I can take a quiet satisfaction
in claiming
that I am not as others are.
Until your voice reminds me
those were the words
the Pharisee spoke
to justify himself.

But as I pause for breath
before continuing my critical assessment
of just how weak I am,
proud, almost, of my own unworthiness,
I hear your voice again
reminding me of good.
Turning me to face the light
of your continuing presence
in my life.
Your grace a greater strength
than all the negatives I feel.

And gently, almost imperceptibly,
your healing starts its work
beneath the bruises
of my self-inflicted hurt.
And I can face myself,
and you, again
in confidence that comes,
not from pretended strength
I know I don't possess,
but from the certainty
of your forgiveness
and the love that says
I can begin again.

The Lord sent Nathan to David. 2 Samuel 12:1

I wonder how Nathan knew the truth about David? His relationship with Bathsheba was obvious of course, since she'd moved into the palace and given birth to their son, but Nathan knew more than that.

Somehow he knew the truth of Uriah's death. Was it just through court gossip, the sort of rumour that would create banner headlines in the tabloid newspapers today? Was Nathan, an acute observer of human frailty, simply putting two and two together and finding the right answer? Or had he heard from Joab, the general who'd had to arrange the betrayal for the king? We might even see it as a revelation although, while not ruling that out, God seems to work more often through our human senses and abilities than in any other way. We simply don't know, and the mechanics of it don't matter as much as the truth behind it all.

What we do know is that nothing can be hidden for ever. For all his power and influence David couldn't keep his wrongdoing secret. In his heart he knew that what he'd done was wrong or he wouldn't have tried to keep it hidden. And even when secrets can for a time be hidden successfully from public view, they are still known to God.

Psalm 139 is a wonderful hymn to this truth:-

'Where can I go from your Spirit? Where can I flee from your presence?' sings the Psalmist. *'If I say, "Surely the darkness will hide me and the light become night around me," even the darkness will not be dark to you; the night will shine like the day, for darkness is as light to you.'*

In earlier days I used to find these words a bit threatening, implying that God was breathing down my neck, looking for the least little transgression, waiting to pounce. Now I see them differently. I rejoice in them because they tell me that God, who is love, is caring for me, overshadowing my every move, watching over me in sheer goodness. The threat becomes a comfort and a source of strength.

And if that seems to contradict what was happening in the confrontation between Nathan and David then we need to look ahead to the denouement. The confrontation was to make David face what he'd done and to bring him back to God, not to extend his punishment. And that's what he wills for each one of us.

Lord, as you dig
below the surface of my life,
removing the accumulated rubbish
of the years,
you bring into the light
so many buried things
I'd rather keep concealed.
The excavation's painful.
Layer after layer stripped back
to show what's underneath.
An archaeology of failure.

And bit by bit
as you unearth
all that lies buried
- no treasure trove -
my first reaction is to hide.
Burrow myself into the dark,
carve out a cave
and for a moment, mole like,
tell myself I'm safe from you.

But you, Lord,
gently relentless in pursuit,
persist in following me,
leaving nowhere to hide.
Your candle flame of truth
may flicker
but it lights my darkness
like the sun at dawn.
And as I'm brought reluctantly
into your light,
blinking, half-blinded
and still struggling,
I find that safety lies
not from but with you.

The pain I feel is therapeutic
and in your burning closeness
lies my healing.
Shine on me, Lord.

'You are the man!' 2 Samuel 12:7

I don't suppose anyone in the palace dared breathe the name of Uriah after Bathsheba had joined David there. We're not told how she got on with his other wives but life seems to have settled down. Until Nathan arrived. Nathan was welcomed by David. He thought well of prophets. It had been the prophet Samuel who had anointed him and supported him so long ago. Prophets were good, until now.

My imagination swings between two pictures of their confrontation. In the first, Nathan stands publicly before David and his whole court, telling his story about the rich man who used his power to steal the poor man's lamb. The story must have stirred powerful emotions in David, taking him back to his early life as a shepherd. A ewe lamb was something to be cared for in those days. Then, when David has committed himself, Nathan's denunciation rang out dramatically for all to hear.

In the second picture, I see David and Nathan in private, Nathan telling his story quietly and persuasively, and looking David in the eye with strong compassion as he faces him with the reality of his sin.

In either scenario the words must have been followed by a profound silence. David the warrior at war with himself as he tried to deal with the avalanche of emotions threatening to overwhelm him. Anger that anyone would dare question what he, the king, had done. Guilt making the anger stronger and hiding behind it. Fear at what this criticism might lead to. Embarrassment and shame to have it all brought out into the open.

I can almost feel David wishing for an instant that he had his spear in his hand to put an end to Nathan - before he remembered Saul and his spear all those years ago.

Something broke in David. His pride shattered, the armour he wore to shield himself from himself fell away, and he saw himself as Nathan saw him, as God saw him. It must have been a bleak moment of utter misery as David saw how far he'd fallen, how distant he was from that young man whose trust in God had been so complete. *'How are the mighty fallen'* - those words from David's elegy for Saul and Jonathan now applied to him.

I hear David whispering to Nathan, 'Is there a way back?' And that was the opportunity God had been waiting for. David unlocked the door and God stepped back into his life as God always will when he's given the invitation.

Someone said, 'When you open the door of your life to God, you find he's already opened the door of his life to you.'

Your truth is fire, Lord.
I think I know how David felt
as he heard
the words the prophet spoke.
Words straight from you.
No comfortable euphemisms
to dress them diplomatically
and make them easier to take.
Truth from the heart of truth itself.
It burns.

Now, while I stand,
a spectator
just watching from the sidelines,
the heat's not too intense.
And though my eyes may sting
in smoke from other people's flames,
I can maintain a distance
and a quiet satisfaction
at their discomfort.

But, Lord, your fire burns too close.
Singes the edges of my life,
then burns me to the core.
Your words are meant
as much for me as him.
There's nothing much to choose
between the two of us.
I've killed no sheep
but Lord I've taken
more than my fair share
of your goodwill.
That's pain enough.

But as I pause and gasp,
the wonder is
your love's a healing flame.
It leaves me scorched but whole.
Your balm may sting
but standing in the ashes
of my failures
I take a breath
and know
that I can start afresh.

Then David said to Nathan, 'I have sinned against the Lord.' Nathan replied, 'The Lord has taken away your sin. You are not going to die.' 2 Samuel 12:13

David made no excuses. He simply acknowledged the wrong he'd done. It's refreshing that he didn't try to blame the woman, Bathsheba. Many men do!

Nathan must have felt a moment of profound relief as he heard the words. He'd challenged the king. It was almost another David and Goliath incident, but this time with David transformed into the powerful villain and Nathan confronting him, armed only with the sling stones of God's truth.

This time though there was no killing. By the laws of the land, which the people believed had been given to them by God, David deserved to die. He'd broken at least three of the ten commandments - by coveting his neighbour's wife, then committing adultery, and finally by murdering her husband. He'd got in pretty deeply, and the penalty for both adultery and murder was death.

David came face to face with what he really was. His power was the facade behind which lived a compromised human being. I don't know when he sang the words we can read in Psalm 51, but they crystallise his feelings at this moment:-

> *'Have mercy on me, O God, according to your unfailing love;*
> *according to your great compassion blot out my transgressions . . .*
> *. . . For I know my transgressions, and my sin is always before me.'*

Then David experienced the wonder of forgiveness. 'The Lord has taken away your sin,' said Nathan. The immediacy takes the breath away. As he repents David sees the face of God's righteous judgement and finds it transformed instantaneously into the face of loving forgiveness.

There are times I find this aspect of God hard to accept. I'd prefer him to punish the sin, especially if it's been committed by someone else. After all that's what they deserve! But the grace of immediate forgiveness is hard to take. And even when I'm the sinner I sometimes feel I could face God a little more easily knowing that I'd paid for what I'd done, but that's not God's way.

His love overrides everything else. Jesus has shown us that.

Lord, is it really true?
The wonder of your love
just takes my breath away.
You leave me gasping.
It simply isn't reasonable to forgive
before exacting retribution.
It goes against the grain
of all the world holds dear.
Punishment should fit the crime,
and if it doesn't change the criminal
then double it.
Debts must be paid,
and when it's someone else
I find it very satisfying
to see them suffer for their sins.

And though it's not a party game,
I'd rather pay a forfeit
when it comes to you and me
so I could claim
I'd earned your favour
rather than take it as a gift.
I find forgiveness freely offered
a humbling experience
beyond anything I've known.
It hurts my pride.
I'd rather pay my way
and buy my round.

It's most unsettling, Lord,
to find that in the instant
that I face myself
and look away in shame
the slate's wiped clean.
Your love obliterates the debt
that stood between us -
although the debt was always my creation,
never yours -
and I'm restored.
Love beyond law and logic overwhelms me.
It can't be analysed,
its depth a mystery too deep to fathom.
I can do nothing but reach out
and hold it close.

'. . . the son born to you will die.' 2 Samuel 12:14

David may have been king but he was also a vulnerable human being. He'd been assured of God's forgiveness for the wrong he'd done but then his son fell ill and it felt as though God was punishing him. And how sad that this child of David and Bathsheba went into Biblical history with no name. As I stand alongside David and Bathsheba in my imagination and feel the helplessness and anguish as they watched their baby sicken and die, I have to ask the same question David must have asked. How could God's forgiveness be real when this was happening?

Guilt doesn't give up easily. It attacks the whole idea of forgiveness in whatever ways it can. What better way than to suggest to David that there was a link between his sin and the baby's suffering, but how wrong.

We need to take a firm hold on the assurances Jesus gives about the overwhelming love and forgiveness of God before we try to interpret incidents like this. Whose fault was it? Why did the child die? Nathan could only understand it as an act of God, a phrase we use so easily and usually wrongly. However much he tried to understand and link them, I'm sure the two events were separate. There was no cause and effect. I have to say honestly - if a little arrogantly - that I couldn't accept a God who would take the life of an innocent baby to punish the parent.

There are so many reasons for children's deaths. Some years ago my work took me to Bhutan, a small kingdom in the Himalayas. There were remote areas in the mountains where almost half the babies born died before they were five years old. This wasn't God's punishment but because the richer Western world hadn't got round to sharing modern medicine with them. Such things aren't caused by God's judgement but our inaction.

Blaming God may make it easier to fit things into the framework of our limited understanding but it doesn't make it true.

In his misery, and I'm sure Bathsheba must have felt the same even though her emotions aren't brought into the picture, David was living through another desert experience, another winter of bleak suffering. The good thing was that it threw him back on God. Again.

A friend of mine said that failure is a doorway to a new encounter with God, and that's what happened with David. He '. . . went into the house of the Lord and worshipped.' (v. 20). David took his turmoil and anguish, his mixed emotions, and offered them to God just as they were.

It may not have solved his problems immediately, but at least it reminded him, and reminds us, of another dimension to life.

*I think I ask too many questions, Lord,
but that's the way I am.
My mind and my imagination
are your gifts to me,
gifts that I treasure
and find joy in using.
And if that means
I need more answers
than you're prepared to give,
I'm sorry,
but I'll go on asking questions anyway.*

*I wonder at the way
your world is organised.
The joys and sorrows,
highs and lows
and all the many happenings in between.
They seem so random,
hitting some and leaving others
apparently untouched.
And when it comes to suffering and death
the textbook answers never satisfy,
ring hollow, echo emptily,
and I am left
still knocking on a door
that never seems to open.*

*Perhaps I ask too much.
I'm sure I do,
and in the end
I know all I can do is trust.
That's what you ask.
That's why, I think,
your silence may be saying more to me
than all that words could say.
But still it's hard
and if I wait,
I wait impatiently
for that great moment when,
my doubts resolved,
my fears removed,
I stand before you
in the splendour of your presence.
No questions left.*

Then David comforted his wife, Bathsheba . . . and she gave birth to a son, and they named him Solomon. The Lord loved him . . .   2 Samuel 12:24

God never gives up on people. Through all the drama of David's life God was there, working away on him. I was going to say 'like a potter with a lump of clay' but I'm not too comfortable with that image. Clay is inert. It's almost totally in the potter's control.

God has created us to be different. We have minds and wills and we can decide for ourselves how we use them and what we do with our lives. Whatever our circumstances there is always a choice. The alternatives may not be to our liking but there's usually more than one way to go.

David was no lump of clay. He was a powerful character with a strong will which helped him survive through turbulent events, even though it led him into deep trouble at times. He got on with life. He'd taken risks, faced difficulties, made decisions. At his best he was clearly conscious of God's presence. At his worst he could turn his back on God, but he never denied his existence, and was sensitive to his mistakes when they were pointed out to him.

And in Solomon's birth David's relationship with God was taken a step further. Solomon - the name has its origin in the word Shalom, *'peace'* - was also named Jedidiah, *'loved by the Lord'*. In Solomon God confirmed the future. He was the son who would consolidate all that David had accomplished, and who would build the Temple David had dreamed of. And an infinitely greater 'Son of David', Jesus, would seal all the purposes God had begun. But that would be much later.

God's purposes are rarely fulfilled instantaneously, although we think we'd like it better if they were. Often the wait is the hardest thing about our relationship with him, but he has his own timing. And he works patiently and slowly through us as he did through David.

His love and forgiveness outlive our restlessness and sin. That doesn't give us an excuse to trespass on his love without regard, it's not a licence to misbehave without thought of consequences, but it is the ultimate reality we cling to. *'Nothing,'* wrote Paul to Christians at Rome, *'nothing will be able to separate us from the love of God that is in Christ Jesus our Lord.'*

Time and again we may stumble as David did, but time and again we are lifted up by the same loving hands, restored to dignity and kinship as children of God.

Lord, when you spoke
of making highways straight,
of cutting down the gradients
on the hills,
and smoothing out rough places
perhaps I didn't understand.
My walk with you
seems diffcrent.
Sometimes I think
I'm travelling in circles
and after all my efforts
I'll be back where I began.

There are smooth roads at times,
I grant you that,
but generally they peter out
or lead to tracks
much rougher than I bargained for.
My breath comes short,
my knees are bruised and cut
from falling
in the rough and stumble
of my daily life.
The valleys I explore are deep
and though the beauty of the mountain beckons,
from where I stand
the climb's so steep.

Then looking back
along the path I've come
I realise
that the journey's not in vain.
Each footstep gained,
in ease or hardship,
brings me nearer to the goal.
And though the far horizon's
blue with mystery
and cloaked in haze,
I know I'm heading in the right direction.
Your presence gives encouragement
and strength to carry on
in certain knowledge
that my journey's end is you,
as its beginning.

. . . Israel's singer of songs.   2 Samuel 23:1

With the birth of Solomon David's life had reached its highest point. Israel had secure borders, a strong army and now an heir who would be king when David died. Perhaps this is the point at which we can leave him.

David could claim many titles. Poet, musician, warrior, king, but the best one was the last he was given, *'Israel's singer of songs'*. And what songs he sang. Songs full of the joy of God's presence; despair when God seemed to withdraw from him. Praise for deliverance from his enemies; impatience when God makes him wait. Anger when he sees the wicked flourish and the innocent suffer. Exultation in victory and wonder at the richness of God's mercy and forgiveness.

In some of his songs David sings of his own righteousness. In others he is deeply ashamed of his sinfulness. Often these conflicting thoughts are part of the same song, one emotion chasing the other, line by line.

Which is the real David? The saint or the sinner? The answer is both because, when the armour is removed, the roles played out and the real David emerges, we see him as a human being. A great man but flawed like the rest of us.

Writing a thousand years later, St. Paul confessed, *'I do not understand what I do. For what I want to do I do not do, but what I hate I do.'* (Romans 7:15). David would have agreed. Throughout his life David lived passionately and struggled with the chaos within, and the only difference between his life and ours is that his was played out on a larger, more dramatic stage. Although our lives are smaller the struggle's just the same.

All the music of human experience and emotion is in his singing, and David played out the harmonies and discords as he awaited the final movement that would lift him into the glory of the full presence of God, the song of his life ended, a new song ready to begin.

Waken my heart, Lord,
to the music of your love.
Help me to sing your song
as David did.
Sometimes he got it wrong
and so do I,
the notes all out of place,
the harmony destroyed.

And then
the melody grows faint,
eludes me altogether,
drowned in the discord
as my life wreaks havoc
with your harmonies.
And in the clash of will
I'm deafened by the silence,
not of your withdrawal,
but of mine.

Then in the loneliness,
the self-created emptiness,
your music comes again.
Your hand plays gently
on the taut strings of my life
offering me a chance
to sing again.

Fine tune me, Lord,
to hear the faintest note you play
and fit my life
around your melodies.
And help me
finally
to recognise
the tune I play is yours.
There all the time
if only I had listened.

Leprosy Mission contact addresses and telephone numbers

International Office:
The Leprosy Mission
80 Windmill Road
Brentford
Middlesex TW8 0QH
UK
Tel: 44 181 569 7292
Fax: 44 181 569 7808
e-mail: friends@tlmint.org
www.leprosymission.org/

TLM Trading Ltd. (for orders):
PO Box 212
Peterborough
PE2 5BR
Tel: 44 1733 239252
Fax: 44 1733 239258
e-mail: TLMTrading@dial.pipex.com

Africa Regional Office:
PO Box H G 893
Highlands
Harare
Zimbabwe
Tel: 263 4 733709
Fax: 263 4 721166
e-mail: tlmiaro@intellisoft.co.zw

Australia:
PO Box 293
Box Hill
Victoria 3128
Tel: 61 398900577
Fax: 61 398900550
e-mail: tlm.aust.nat@c031.aone.net.au

Belgium:
PO Box 20
1800 Vilvoorde
Tel/Fax: 32 22519983

Canada:
75 The Donway West, Suite 1410
North York
Ontario M3C 2E9
Tel: 1 416 4413618
Fax: 1 416 4410203
e-mail: tlm@tlmcanada.org

Denmark:
Skindergade 29 A, 1.,
1159 Copenhagen
Tel: 45 331 18642
Fax: 45 331 18645
e-mail: lepra@post3.tele.dk

England and Wales, Channel Islands & The Isle of Man:
Goldhay Way
Orton Goldhay
Peterborough PE2 5GZ
Tel: 44 1733 370505
Fax: 44 1733 370960
e-mail: post@tlmew.org.uk

Finland:
Hakolahdentie 32A4
00200 Helsinki
Tel: 358 9692 3690
Fax: 358 9692 4323

France:
BP 186
63204 Riom Cedex
Tel/Fax: 33 473 387660

Germany:
Kuferstrasse 12
73728 Esslingen
Tel: 49 711 353 072
Fax: 49 711 350 8412
e-mail: LEPRA-Mission@t-online.de

Hong Kong:
GPO Box 380
Central
Tel: 852 2805 6362
Fax: 852 2805 6397
e-mail: tlmhk@netvigator.com

Hungary:
Alagi Ter 13
Budapest 1151

India Regional Office:
CNI Bhavan
16 Pandit Pant Marg
New Delhi 110 001
Tel: 91 11 3716920
Fax: 91 11 3710803
e-mail: tlmindia@del2.vsnl.net.in

Italy:
Via Rismondo 10A
05100 Terni
Tel/Fax: 39 0744 811218
e-mail: arpe@seinet.it

Netherlands:
Postbus 902
7301 BD Apeldoorn
Tel: 31 553558535
Fax: 31 553554772
e-mail: leprazending.nl@inter.nl.net

New Zealand:
PO Box 10-227
Auckland 1004
Tel: 64 9 630 2818
Fax: 64 9 630 0784
e-mail: tlmnz@clear.net.nz

Northern Ireland:
Leprosy House
44 Ulsterville Avenue
Belfast BT9 7AQ
Tel: 44 1232 381937
Fax: 44 1232 381842
e-mail: 106125.167@compuserve.com

Norway:
c/o Bistandsnemnd
PO Box 2347 Solli
Arbingst. 11
0201 Oslo
Tel: 47 22438110
Fax: 47 22438730
e-mail: bistandn@online.no

Portugal:
Casa Adelina
Sítio do Poio
8500 Portimão
Tel: 351 82 471180
Fax: 351 82 471516
e-mail: coaa@telepac.pt

Republic of Ireland:
5 St James Terrace
Clonskeagh Road
Dublin 6
Tel/Fax: 353 126 98804
e-mail: 106125.365@compuserve.com

Scotland:
89 Barnton Street
Stirling FK8 1HJ
Tel: 44 1786 449266
Fax: 44 1786 449766
e-mail: lindatodd@compuserve.com

SEA Regional Office:
6001 Beach Road
#08-06 Golden Mile Tower
199589 Singapore
Tel: 65 294 0137
Fax: 65 294 7663
e-mail: pdsamson@tlmsea.com.sg

Southern Africa:
Private Bag X06
Lyndhurst 2106
Johannesburg
Tel: 27 11 440 6323
Fax: 27 11 440 6324
e-mail: Leprosy@infonet.co.za

Spain:
C/Beneficencia, 18 Bis-1°
28004 Madrid
Tel/Fax: 34 915945105
e-mail: mundosolidari@mx3.redestb.es

Sweden:
Box 145
692 23 Kumla
Tel: 46 19 583790
Fax: 46 19 583741
e-mail: lepra@algonet.se

Switzerland:
Chemin de Réchoz
1027 Lonay/VD
Tel: 41 21 8015081
Fax: 41 21 8031948

Zimbabwe:
PO Box BE200
Belvedere
Harare
Tel: 263 4 741817
e-mail: tlmzim@tlmzim.icon.co.zw

ALM International:
1 ALM Way
Greenville
S C 29601
U.S.A.
Tel: 1 864 537 7679
Fax: 1 864 271 7062
e-mail: amlep@leprosy.org

The Leprosy Mission Response Card

Eddie Askew is a popular Christian author, artist and retreat leader. The Leprosy Mission receive funds from the sale of his books to help people affected by leprosy. They are available from The Leprosy Mission in your own country or from TLM Trading Limited in the UK:-

TLM Trading Limited, owned by The Leprosy Mission, creates jobs for people affected by leprosy. Their goods are sold in a catalogue along with gifts, cards and the Eddie Askew books to raise funds for The Leprosy Mission.

Title	Order Code
A Silence and a Shouting	03001
Disguises of Love	C3002
Many Voices One Voice	03003
No Strange Land	03004
Facing the Storm	03005
Breaking the Rules	03006
Cross Purposes	03000
Slower than Butterflies (book)	03024
Slower than Butterflies (audio cassette)	20200
Music on the Wind	03025

Please send me information about:- (please tick)

☐ The Leprosy Mission's mail order catalogue.
☐ The Leprosy Mission's work.
☐ Prayer support.
☐ Sending a regular gift by automatic payment, standing order, or direct debit to support The Leprosy Mission.
☐ Tax efficient ways of supporting The Leprosy Mission.
☐ Service Overseas with The Leprosy Mission.

Credit Card Sales and enquiries: Tel: 01733 239252 Fax: 01733 239258

Title .... Initials .... Surname ....

Address ....

....

Postcode .... Country ....

Source Code 250

Postcard

TLM Trading Limited
P.O. Box 212
Peterborough
PE2 5GD
United Kingdom

Please use your local Leprosy Mission address if you prefer

MINNESOTA MAYHEM

A HISTORY OF

CALAMITOUS EVENTS,
HORRIFIC ACCIDENTS,
DASTARDLY  DREADFUL
CRIME BEHAVIOR
in the Land of
TEN THOUSAND LAKES

BEN WELTER

THE
History
PRESS

Published by The History Press
Charleston, SC 29403
www.historypress.net

First published 2012
Second printing 2012
Third printing 2012
Fourth printing 2013

Manufactured in the United States

ISBN 978.1.60949.597.8

Library of Congress CIP data applied for.

CONTENTS

CONTENTS

INTRODUCTION

The first edition of the *Minneapolis Tribune* hit the streets in May 1867. Virtually every page of every issue of the *Tribune* and its descendants is preserved on microfilm stored in steel cabinets at the *Star Tribune* in downtown Minneapolis. During dinner breaks, I head to the newsroom library, fish out one of the hundreds of rolls, thread it into a digital reader and take a look back in time. How much did it cost to block and clean a bowler hat in 1898? How did the *Tribune* cover the sinking of the *Titanic*? What movies were showing in Hennepin Avenue theaters in the 1950s? Did St. Paul's "super mayor" of the early '70s, Charlie McCarty, really use an electronic device to turn traffic lights in his favor?

The most interesting pieces find new life in my blog, "Yesterday's News" (www.startribune.com/yesterday). Since 2005, I've posted five hundred stories and more than one thousand photos. Fresh interviews and reader recollections flesh out many of the posts.

Minnesota Mayhem, based on my blog, is a collection of some of the state's worst moments—large and small, tragic and amusing, heartbreaking and revelatory—over the past 140 years. These newspaper accounts are preserved in their original form, along with photos from the archives of the Minnesota Historical Society, Hennepin County Library's Minneapolis Collection, the Carlton County Historical Society and the *Star Tribune*.

I hope you enjoy these voices from Minnesota's past.

A CON MAN WITHOUT PEER

*P*osing as a wealthy Scottish landowner, a well-groomed gentleman identifying himself as Lord Gordon-Gordon arrived in Minnesota in August 1871. Using money stolen in an earlier swindle in Edinburgh, he deposited $40,000 in cash at the National Exchange Bank in Minneapolis and checked into the Nicollet Hotel. In conversations around town, he mentioned in offhanded fashion that he was an heir of the earls of Gordon and had an annual income of more than $1 million. He also let it be known that he was interested in buying fifty thousand acres of Minnesota land on which to resettle tenants of his overpopulated estates.

Word of the wealthy foreigner quickly spread in the city of twenty thousand, and within days, Gordon-Gordon met with Colonel John Loomis, a Northern Pacific Railway official who invited him to join rail executives and surveyors on a tour of the state. The men traveled in high style. According to the Fergus Falls Daily Journal, the caravan featured "forty horses, twelve men to pitch tents, a French cook and a number of colored waiters wearing white linen aprons and white silk gloves." Gordon-Gordon insisted that everyone address him as "My Lord." The railroad provided him with a private carriage, a secretary and a valet—and covered all his expenses during the lavish, three-month tour, at a cost estimated at $15,000.

"He is the richest landlord in Europe," a beaming Loomis told Northern Pacific directors. "He will invest $500,000,000 with us."

William A. Croffut, who was editor of the Minneapolis Tribune in the early 1870s, later described the tour in Putnam's Magazine:

The details of Lord Gordon-Gordon's early life and his real identity remain unclear. Two things are certain: he was neither a Scotsman nor an heir to the earls of Gordon.

His Lordship saw the State thoroughly, and inspected and selected vast areas of arable land that would rejoice the soul of a Highlander. He also incidentally located and named several cities, explaining that it would be necessary to have churches and schools well organized before his colonists would flock thither in large numbers. Then he said he was satisfied and the excursion could now halt while he went to New York for money to pay for his purchase. While up at Oak Lake, he had borrowed "a little change" from Col. Loomis—it is not known exactly how much. Then the excursion retired to Minneapolis, freighted with great expectations. Lord Gordon deftly lifted his $40,000 out of [the National Exchange Bank], partook of a banquet *au revoir* and vanished from the sight of his dear Minnesota friends—carrying with him incidentally a letter of warm introduction from Colonel Loomis to Horace Greeley.

Gordon-Gordon next materialized in New York in January 1872. He rented a suite at the luxurious Metropolitan Hotel, where he was visited by the city's social and economic elite, including Greeley, editor of the New York Tribune. *In this new circle of friends, Gordon-Gordon was now suggesting he had an annual income of $3 million and, through his European connections, controlled $30 million in Erie Railway stock. Word of his interest in Erie soon reached Jay Gould, the wealthy speculator who was struggling to maintain command of the railroad. The two agreed to join forces, and Gould gave Gordon-Gordon the $500,000 in cash and stock needed to secure control of the Erie board.*

The deception was soon revealed, and all of the money and most of the stock were recovered. On April 9, Gould had Gordon-Gordon arrested on charges of felonious sale of the remaining stock. Several wealthy New Yorkers put up $37,000 in bail money, allowing him to remain free until trial. But before the case reached court, his lordship disappeared. On April 16, the Minneapolis Tribune, *for the first time, hinted that Gordon-Gordon might not be what he seemed:*

Left: Horace Greeley. *Courtesy of the Library of Congress.*

Right: Jay Gould. *Courtesy of the Library of Congress.*

Lord Gordon, who was arrested in New York the other day at the instance of Jay Gould, and who gave bail to answer the charges made, is reported to have absconded. From all accounts, he appears to have played a most successful confidence game, deceiving completely such men as Jay Gould, Thomas A. Scott, Horace Greeley and others equally well known. He is reported to have made from $200,000 to $300,000 by his operations. The beautiful and accomplished lady who, as his wife, occupied his costly residence on Staten Island, is also among the missing.

Gordon-Gordon turned up in Minnesota on April 30, trying to reclaim "a span of valuable horses" he had left in St. Paul and "put to blush those who have believed the recent rumors that he was an adventurer." He didn't stay long. On May 17, he was back in New York, taking the stand to answer questions in the case of Gould v. Gordon. *Gould's lead attorney pressed him on his family background, and Gordon-Gordon provided what turned out to be fictitious names and addresses of a purported stepfather, sister, brother-in-law and uncle. Overnight, Gould's representatives checked on the information and found it to be false. Gordon-Gordon checked out of the Metropolitan on May 22, leaving no forwarding address, and failed to appear at his next court date that week.*

He resurfaced a month later. "In the suit of Gould against Lord Gordon," the Minneapolis Tribune *reported on June 21, "his lordship unexpectedly appeared as* *a witness." His lawyer assured the New York court that Gordon-Gordon would never have been absent if the conditions of his attendance had been rightly understood. Gordon-Gordon apologized for the misunderstanding and then quietly answered the questions of counsel, giving what turned out to be a fictional account of the source of his Erie stock. He was released on his bond of $1,000 and retired, "via a two dollar hack," to his hotel. He returned to court the next day, testifying at length about his dealings with Gould. The case was adjourned until September 3. But by then Gordon-Gordon, sensing the end of his good fortune in the United States, was long gone, his whereabouts unknown.*

In the summer of 1873, two Minnesotans spotted the bogus nobleman in Fort Garry, Manitoba, and alerted Minneapolis mayor George Brackett, a friend of one of the bail bondsmen with a financial interest in returning Gordon-Gordon to New York. The mayor dispatched two policemen to accompany a representative of the bondsman on a mission to capture Gordon-Gordon and bring him to justice.

Things did not go as planned. The Minneapolis Tribune *of July 8 reported the particulars of the thoroughly botched affair:*

THE TAKERS TOOK.
CAPTURE AND RELEASE OF LORD GORDON-GORDON
MIKE HOY AND OWEN KEEGAN IN FELONS' CELLS.
HON. FLETCHER CARRIED TO FORT GARRY IN IRONS.
HE APPEALS PATHETICALLY FOR IMMEDIATE ASSISTANCE.
GEO. N. MERRIAM IN DANGER—J.C. BURBANK MAKES TRACKS.
MAYOR BRACKETT AND MAJOR LOCHREN ALLEGED ACCESSORIES.
"BE IT EVER SO HUMBLE, THERE'S NO PLACE LIKE HOME."

Something over a year ago, Gordon Gordon—otherwise known as Lord Gordon—had a financial difficulty with the notorious Jay Gould, which resulted in My Lord being held to bail in the sum of $37,500. The late Horace F. Clark, the well known railroad manager and speculator in stocks, took stock in Gordon, and, with other friends, became his surety. Gordon, it is generally conceded, could have worsted Gould in a stand-up fight, but acting on the principle that "he who fights and runs away, may live to fight another day," he suddenly concluded New York had no charms for him, and left his bondsmen in the lurch. They called him pet names, and names which do not come under that head, but it availed nothing—he didn't wish to return. He made his way to Manitoba and made a homestead near the dismal looking walls of Fort Garry, where he has since remained.

A few weeks ago Mr. Clark died, and his heirs concluded that they would not lose the half of $37,500 if they could help it. Ascertaining his supposed whereabouts they procured what is known as a bail-piece, and appointed an agent to bring Lord Gordon into their presence. Lawyers assert that a bail-piece is a document that will hold water every time—that the principle that a bail may surrender his principal and take him wherever he can be found is one of common law, and has been repeatedly affirmed, not only in English courts, but in our own, and that the decisions are all one way on this question.

Be that as it may, the agent in question (he may as well be called Smith—John Smith—the name having slipped the name of the reporter) came hither, and secured the services of Michael Hoy (the policeman who was so missed in the East Division on the Fourth) to aid him in making the arrest. Smith and Hoy, with instructions how to proceed, left Minneapolis nearly two weeks ago, and have not yet returned. Neither has Owen Keegan, Hoy's left bower.

Sheriff Johnson [of Minneapolis] made preparations on Saturday to accommodate a distinguished guest [Gordon], but the distinguished guest cometh not—whether he will, remains to be seen. The reasons for his not putting in an appearance will, by reference to the following, "more fully and at large appear."

Hoy was instructed to arrest Gordon, and with the aid of a Mr. Bentley (Smith remaining at Pembina), did so at an early hour Thursday morning, and gave him a hurried ride towards Pembina. Two miles more, and the party would have been on American soil, but they have yet to travel those two additional miles, for just about that time a squad of men dressed in the uniform of Manitoba infantry, and acting as body guard to the police, arrested the redoubtable Hoy and released the prisoner he had journeyed so far to capture. But they stopped not here. Having heard of Mike's fighting qualities— how he was considered almost equal to a whole regiment—they loaded him down with a blacksmith shop [in other words, put him in manacles] and marched him back (to wagon) to the Fort.

Did the blood-thirsty red-coats stop there? Not they. Loren Fletcher, one of our distinguished representatives to the Legislature, happened to be in that neighborhood, and was telegraphed to remain until Maj. Brackett arrived [Hoy went in his place] and did so. After the arrest of Hoy and Bentley, Mr. Fletcher and Geo. N. Merriam were arrested as accessories, J.C. Burbank making remarkably quick time across the line. What became of Keegan, report saith not; perhaps "Bentley" is the same individual.

Whatever fault may lie at the door of our neighbors beyond the disputed boundary line, no one can charge them with partiality. Having loaded Hoy as aforesaid, they manacled the others to match. Whether the Minnesota Legislature will declare war for the indignity thus offered to one of its members, it is too early to decide. Probably not. But facts are stubborn things, and the facts stand out prominently that the Hon. Loren Fletcher was carried to Fort Garry in irons; that he was accompanied by the other gentlemen referred to; and that at the latest accounts they were languishing in a British Bastile, with no George Francis Train to make their keepers tremble. "'Tis true, 'tis pity, and pity 'tis 'tis true."

Mr. Fletcher was not accustomed to such treatment, and it made him nervous. As soon as he could get a chance he telegraphed to friends here: "In jail. For --'s sake come to our rescue. St. Paul is no comparison. If you can't come send us some cigars." This dispatch was received Saturday afternoon, and Mayor Geo. A. Brackett, ex-Mayor Eugene M. Wilson, Hon. Wm. Lochren and others arranged to rescue him or perish in the attempt. They left here in a special train, consisting of engine, tender and one car, and reached Moorhead at ten o'clock the next morning, the fastest time on record over this route—thirty miles an hour. A telegram from Mr. Lochren announces the arrival of the party at Pembina [in present-day North Dakota, two miles south of the border] at four o'clock yesterday afternoon, and that they will reach for Garry early this morning, "when the fun will commence."

J.W. Taylor, U.S. Consul, telegraphed to Lochren, McNair & Gilfillan, attorneys for the parties who desire to interview Gordon[,] that the Attorney General of Manitoba expressed a doubt as to the rights of Hoy's army to take Gordon out of Canada, owing to the provisions of the Ashburton treaty, to which the reply was sent that the treaty had been examined and that in the opinion of the attorneys it did not apply.

The hearing will take place to-day, unless the same be continued on some pretext of Gordon, and as Manitoba is a law unto itself, it is useless to prophesy as to the result. Merriam will come back. Hoy and Keegan will return. Fletcher will sing

"Home again, home again,
From a foreign shore,
And oh, it fills my heart with joy,
To greet my friends once more."

But when? "Aye, there's the rub." Possibly within a few days. Probably within a few weeks. Perhaps not for months. Who can tell? Hope bids us be cheerful, but who can be cheerful under such circumstances? We pause for a reply.

The report left out a few important questions. The biggest: Why didn't the Minneapolis policemen, armed with a legal document attesting to their authority to arrest Gordon, work with Manitoba officials to secure his capture? It's clear that the Americans weren't convinced the "bail-piece" was valid. To the outraged citizens of Minnesota, however, that was of little concern, and within days, the arrests had become a full-blown international dispute. Some Minnesota newspapers called for a militia to be raised to rescue the Americans. Mayor Brackett, unsuccessful in pressing for the men's release in Fort Garry, later joined Governor Horace Austin for meetings with President Ulysses Grant and Secretary of State Hamilton Fish in Washington and New Jersey.

Diplomatic pressure eventually forced the Manitoba court to accept what amounted to a plea deal. On September 16, more than two months after their arrest, the Americans admitted to reduced charges and were sentenced to twenty-four hours in jail each.

What happened to Gordon-Gordon? "My Lord" was still at large, outside the reach of U.S. law. By now he was being referred to in newspapers from Minneapolis to London as an impostor, a thief, a liar, a plunderer and a "pestiferous blackguard." His pursuers, including the victim of his first big con, a jeweler in Edinburgh, Scotland, where he had been known as Lord Glencairn, patiently tracked him down and worked through government channels to secure his extradition properly. On August 1, 1874, he was arrested at a cottage in Headingly, Manitoba. The Minneapolis Tribune *of August 4 described the final chapter in the strange case of Lord Gordon-Gordon:*

THE END OF GORDON GORDON.
HE PUTS A PERIOD TO HIS OWN EXISTENCE.
AND ROBS JUSTICE OF A JUST SACRIFICE.
HE IS CRAFTY TO THE LAST.
[Special Telegram.]

FORT GARRY, Aug. 3.—The last scene in the notorious Lord Gordon-Gordon drama was wound up last Saturday night with a

Wherever he went, Lord Gordon-Gordon—also known as Lord Glencairn, Honorable Mr. Herbert Hamilton, George Herbert Gordon, George Hubert Smith and John Herbert Charles Gordon—arrived in style.

tragic epilogue. Detective Monroe, of Toronto, arrived here a short time ago on the steamer *International*, armed with two warrants issued by Police Magistrate McNab, of Toronto, which were also endorsed by the Stipendary Magistrate here, Gilbert McMincker. One of the warrants was based on the information of Marshall & Son, jewelers, of Edinburgh, Scotland, accusing Gordon of obtaining goods on false pretenses. The second warrant accused him of bringing stolen goods into Canada.

Doctor Monroe in company with Lawyer Bann, who acted for Marshall & Son, and two local policemen, proceeded on Saturday afternoon to Headingly, arriving in the evening, and went direct to Gordon's lodgings at Mrs. Corbett's, when Monroe made the arrest without meeting with resistance and before several witnesses. Gordon manifested much self-possession and calmly asked if this was another kidnapping affair. He received sufficient assurance that it was not, and requested that he might not be taken through the States on learning of the legality and regularity of the arrest.

He was also desirous of changing the suit he had on at the time for heavier wearing apparel, and the officer removed the handcuffs for that purpose.

He went to the foot of his bed with Monroe following him closely, and pretending to look for his Scotch cap, seized upon a pistol and exclaiming, "I will not go a step further," he thrust the pistol up to his right ear and fired, expiring almost instantly.

An inquest is at present being held at Headingly, sixteen miles away, and the excitement here is considerable.

FIRE DESTROYS THE STATE CAPITOL

MARCH 2, 1881, *MINNEAPOLIS TRIBUNE*

*O*n a winter's evening in 1881, a fire broke out at the State Capitol in St. Paul while both houses were in session. Hundreds fled down the building's single stairway as flames raced overhead and smoke filled the chambers. The building was destroyed. And yet, aside from a "one-armed janitor" who was hit in the head by a burning timber while trying to haul books to safety, no one was injured.

    This riveting account appeared on the Tribune's front page the next day under an exhaustive bank of headlines. Miraculously, the word "miraculously" appears just once in the story.

In Ashes

The State Capitol in St. Paul Burned Last Evening.

The Structure Totally Destroyed, with Many Valuable Records.

Over Eleven Thousand Books of the State Library Burned.

The Valuable Collection of the Academy of Sciences Lost.

The Building Valued at $80,000—Other Losses Beyond Estimation.

Narrow Escape from a Far More Terrible Disaster.

Both Bodies in Session When the Fire Broke Out.

Scenes of Great Excitement—Members Escaping by Windows.

Cause of the Fire Unknown—Hints at Incendiarism.

An Extra Session Made Necessary—Scenes and Incidents.

Arrangements for the Meeting of the Two Houses To-day.

In the early days of the *Minneapolis Tribune*, news headlines competed for attention with ads for furniture, groceries and books.

A Cindered Capitol.

Special Telegram to The Tribune.

St. Paul, March 1.—The burning of the state capitol building last evening, upon the very eve of the close of the legislative session, is a misfortune the extent of which cannot at this time be fully appreciated. The calamity is so sudden a one, and the excitement which followed the escape of at least 300 people by a single stairway, from a building suddenly, mysteriously and almost entirely enveloped in flames, is so intense that the coolest reporter cannot measure the calamity.

The Fire Broke Out
at about a quarter past 9 o'clock. Both branches of the legislature were busy with the immense amount of work which had accumulated, and the galleries and lobbies were crowded with an unusually large number of people. The senate was busily grinding away at house bills, and had almost completed that order, and the attendance in that branch was large in anticipation of reaching the bond bill, the amendments to which had to be concurred in by that branch. With a suddenness which is beyond description, and almost entirely beyond appreciation, the members of both branches were apprised of the fact that

the Building Was on Fire;
that the flames threatened to shut off escape by the only stairway with which the building is supplied, and that an appalling calamity stared at the lowest estimate 300 people in the face. The scene in the senate, where The Tribune reporter was on duty, was an exciting one, and not soon to be forgotten. The lieutenant-governor was in

the chair, and the secretary calling bills upon their third reading, the sawdust memorial just having been reached. The senators were variously occupied in their seats, or lounging about in the smoking-room, when some one burst into the room and shouted "fire," and

A PERFECT PANDEMONIUM OF SHOUTS

followed. The alarm needed no further proof than was apparent to every person in the room. Through the windows at the back of the gallery it was evident that a great sheet of flame held possession of the hallway or corridor into which the main and only stairway leads. There was a grand rush for the doors, the lieutenant-governor, with admirable coolness, attempting to allay the excitement, which only rose the higher as a body of senators attempted to escape by the door, only to be

BEATEN BACK BY FLAME,

and a cloud of black smoke that threatened to shut off that escape. Brave men blanched with fear. A thousand thoughts rushed through excited minds, and the distance from the windows to the ground was measured with anxious eyes. "Shut the doors!" "Shut the doors!" "Don't make a draft!" "Act like men!" yelled the excited crowd, who rushed about the room measuring every possible mode of escape. "Some one should

MOVE TO ADJOURN,"

shouted the secretary, and senator Crooks made the motion, which was put and responded to with an unanimity of sentiment not usually encountered. The doors were closed, but a second attempt revealed the fact that the cloud of smoke had raised somehow, and a pell-mell dash was made for the stairs, down which the members of the house and the spectators in the gallery were already passing. Meanwhile some of the occupants of the senate chamber, among them Senators Pillsbury, Officer, Miller, Assistant Clerk Wedge and The Globe and Tribune reporters had escaped, by the window to the veranda at the east end of the building, where they were engaged in

YELLING LUSTILY

for ladders and ropes. The escape was none too soon, for before the last person had left the room a great cloud of flame enveloped the dome of the building, had spread through the tinder-box mansard-roof and great cinders were dropping though the ventilator into the center of the senate chamber, where a fire was kindled in the carpet. A few of the senators had the presence of mind to save their effects, nearly all of them bundled into their wraps, and the clerks with admirable coolness and presence of mind

RESCUED ALL THEIR RECORDS,

the bills in the pigeon-holes of their desks and everything of value upon which they could lay their hands. They were the last to leave the room, carrying with them the uncompleted legislation, the fruit of months of consideration. Several intrepid members returned by the window later and secured other of their effects, but less than three minutes had elapsed before all the upper portion of the building was enveloped in flames and the structure was doomed.

THE SCENE IN THE HOUSE

was even more exciting. The first premonition of danger was the dropping of fire into the gallery, a shout from the resort of the vox populi of Fire! and the bursting into the room of a cloud of black, sickening and forbidding smoke. Two hundred persons rose as one individual, Mr. Rice, who was in the chair, deserting his seat unceremoniously. Those who first attempted it, believed escape by the long narrow hall, more than one hundred feet in length, presented to them what appeared to be

AN INSURMOUNTABLE BARRIER.

Mr. Denny, with more coolness than some others, jumped to the speaker's desk and cautioned the crowd to go, but to do it with discretion and coolness; that the passage was open; but an unknown influence suddenly, and for a brief interval, cleared the hall of smoke, and the mass of humanity, among who were a number of ladies, poured down the hall an excited, eager and unmanageable crowd. Miraculously no one was hurt, and every person escaped, though more than one occupant of the room counted the cost of a leap for life through the window, and philosophically made up his mind that a great danger was to be met. The scene was

TRAGIC AND HUMOROUS,

and never to be forgotten by the eye-witnesses of it. Men, usually calm, dashed wildly about the room, a thousand terrible fancies flashing through their brains. Only one member, Mr. Schmidt,

Minnesota's first Capitol, shown here about eight years before the fire, was built in 1853 at Tenth and Cedar Streets in St. Paul. *Courtesy of the Hennepin County Library, Minneapolis Collection.*

of Washington county, concluded to jump rather than brave an uncertain battle with the flames, and dropped from one of the windows into a snowbank, with only a few unimportant bruises. The clerks, appreciating their responsibility, gathered together the records and carried them to a place of safety. Speaker Fletcher, with an eye to the danger that threatened the younger pages, took them

UNDER HIS PERSONAL CARE,

and dragged them with him out of the building. The spectacle which met the eye of the crowd as they escaped into the free air of safety was a building, the roof of which was almost entirely enveloped in flames, and the dome of which was a great beacon of light, spreading a lurid glare over the entire city.

THE ORIGIN OF THE FIRE

is wrapped in some mystery. There were no premonitory evidences of the fire. When it was first discovered it seemed to have gained full sway throughout the range of the entire French roof. It seemed to have gained more headway in the dome of the building, and is variously ascribed to the explosion of gas in that part of the building and to an incendiary. The janitors hold to the latter theory. There was no gas lit or lights of any kind in the garrets, which are apparently nearly ten feet in heighth in the center, and extending over the entire building, a structure nearly 300 feet in length, and of a width ranging from 50 feet to 150 feet. Half an hour had not elapsed before the whole second story was enveloped.

THE LOSS.

The loss is beyond estimation. The structure was worth not less than $80,000, and contained the accumulation of years, which cannot be replaced. On the first or ground floor the valuables were placed in the vaults or removed from the building, the carpets in some of the rooms even being removed. The most serious loss, undoubtedly, is the state library, which contained 12,580 volumes, many of which cannot be replaced. Less than 1,000 of the entire number were saved. The money value of the library was probably $75,000, but it does not express the real value of the property. The treasury vault contained $2,190,000 of state and Missouri bonds, besides other valuable property, and towards this receptacle the

FIRST STREAMS WERE TURNED

and were not permitted to cease. The state's property is probably safe. The insurance across the hall was supplied with a vault, and the secretary of state's room and the auditor's department, with a like safe depository, and nearly all other departments with safes. Such property as could be placed in these receptacles is probably safe, but as soon as it was evident that the lower floor could be entered with safety a steady stream of men were engaging in carrying away the contents of the building. The records of the supreme court clerk's office were carried out, and when last seen by The Tribune reporter were dumped on the snow in front of the burning building. Secretary Williams, of

THE HISTORICAL SOCIETY,

took personal supervision of the removal of the valuable and not-to-be-replaced articles in his department, which were carried to the Universalist church, opposite the capitol. Nearly everything not securely deposited in the vault was removed. The Academy of Science, which occupied a room in the basement beyond that of the Historical Society, did not fare so well. In the confusion the key to the room was lost, and before the door could be broken open the smoke drove back the workers. A very valuable collection of natural curiosities is therefore lost. The reports of the departments, the accumulation of years in the state department, were stored in the basement also, and

ARE ALL DESTROYED,

and so far as could be learned many valuable documents in the adjutant-general's office. The state officials have confidence in their respective vaults preserving the essential documents in their stands, so that the record of government may be maintained without serious interruption. But the disaster precipitates

an Extra Session

of the legislature, although steps were taken promptly during the evening by the mayor and lieutenant-governor and speaker for the legislature to resume its session this morning in the new market building, which will at once be placed in readiness for occupancy. The senate is to meet this morning in the municipal court room in that structure, and the house of representatives in another apartment, known as Market Hall. The various departments of state are to be distributed throughout the first floors, in the stalls, fully separated by glass partitions. It is a fortunate fact that a building so well fitted for the purpose created by the necessity is not yet occupied, and is so near completion. The clerks of the two branches were busily engaged last evening in

Straightening Out Their Records,

preparatory to the resumption of business to-day, but it is not anticipated that much will be accomplished, with only another working-day and business in a chaotic condition. There is but one opinion and that is that the government will promptly call an extra session, that provision may be made for temporary quarters for the state departments, and for rebuilding the present structure or some new one. The fire department battled bravely with the flames, but the streams were not many in number nor of notable power. They made no impression whatever, apparently, on the flames, which licked up the combustible interior of the building, leaving the stark walls at 2 o'clock this morning lit up with the embers of the fire. Crowds of people assembled during the progress of the fire. Later in the evening the persons who were in the building when the fire broke out, principally excited solons, gathered in groups and recited their narrow escapes and incidents of

a Memorable Night,

which threatened to be crowded with horror and tragic events. "I had made up my mind," said Col. L.L. Baxter, "that my time had come, and said as much to Mr. Dunn. I've been in tight places before, but never in one that seemed to threaten so sure a fate as that for a few minutes." The eight or ten ladies in the hall of the house of representatives were almost frantic in their fear and were calmed with difficulty. Senator Hinds promptly took into his care the single lady in the senate chamber, who was engaged in conversation with him when the alarm was first given, and led her in safety out of the building. They were among the first to brave the flames in the hallway.

A number of the members in their haste to escape from the building left their hats and coats, and though some of them were searching for the lost garments among a number taken out by the ladder brigade, numbers will measure their chief loss in this direction. The only insurance on any of the property that has been discovered is that of $10,000 in the London, Liverpool & Globe, placed against the policy of the state upon the library. It will be but

A DROP IN THE BUCKET

in replacing the property. It has been for years, as was developed at the time of the fire at St. Peter, the theory that the state can best afford to insure its own property. The subject of placing insurance on the capital building was broached recently in one of the legislative committees, but did not meet with favor or approval. Unity church, the Lutheran church, Judge Palmer's residence and other contiguous buildings were made storehouses during the early evening, but at this writing, 1 o'clock, a force of men are engaged in removing the department records and furniture into the market house, where some of the officials expect to be prepared for business at the regular hour. The halls were being made in readiness for the assembling of the two branches of the legislature at 10 o'clock. Among the books discovered to have been saved from the library are a set of old English reports, among the most valuable in the collection.

A HEROIC EFFORT

was made by Chas. Chappel, the one-armed janitor of the capitol building, to save more of this collection, the value of which he was quick to appreciate, and he lingered in the room until a burning timber fell, striking him on the head. He left then, but carried under his single arm all the books he could conveniently and successfully grasp. Gov. Pillsbury, who was not in the city last evening, but he had a conversation by telephone with Mayor Dawson, of this city, who promptly tendered the market house, and whom he desired to proceed and make whatever arrangement for the resumption of business as his judgment and generosity dictated. For some unaccountable reason the bond bill was

LINKED WITH THE HINTS AT INCENDIARISM,
but that theory is thoroughly preposterous. Had any designing person desired to wipe out at this stage that portion of the minutes the work could have been more thoroughly accomplished after the bodies had adjourned for the night. But Secretary Jennison, appreciating the importance of that bill, made it the object of his special attention in his effort to save. The most reasonable theory of the fire is that some careless person dropped in the space between the ceiling and dome

A LIGHTED CIGAR
that started a fire among the cobwebbed rafters of the old and thoroughly seasoned tinder-box. The place is not accessible to the general public. And Jefferson Davis Hudson, the very much eulogized flag-raiser, elected though the efforts of W.D. Rice, has been almost the only person to pass through that part of the building to the dome. He was up there, it is stated, about an hour before the fire broke out, and alleges that he discovered no evidence of fire, and professes total ignorance of its cause. The rapidity of its spread is one of the mysterious features of the disaster, and had there been an explosion, of which there was no evidence, the conflagration might be attributed to escaping gas accumulating in that unventilated apart of the building, and igniting; but the generally accepted theory is that the fire was

INCENDIARY IN CHARACTER,
and near as can be stated was ignited over the senate chamber, if it was not set in more than one place, with what intent beyond cussedness no person can say. Access to the attic and dome was through the gallery of the senate chamber.

Among the valuables known to have been lost was the large painting, belonging to Mrs. Loemans, of St. Anthony Falls in 1821, which had been deposited in the senate chamber. The picture of Gen. Sherman, also in that part of the building, was burned. The life-size picture of Gen. Thomas that hung in the house of representatives was saved. Mrs. Loeman's picture was a rare one, and cannot be replaced.

At 2 o'clock this morning the fire is simply smouldering, and a force of men is engaged in establishing the departments of state in the market house.

JUDGE COOLEY'S COURTROOM

DECEMBER 3, 1882, *MINNEAPOLIS MORNING TRIBUNE*

A *slice of judicial life from the* Morning Tribune:

A SCENE IN THE MUNICIPAL COURT.

Three lads, ranging in age from 10 to 15 years, were brought into the municipal court Friday, charged with the larceny of five handsleds. The lads were arraigned and admitted their guilt to the extent of one sled each. They were sent into an anteroom and the business of the court proceeded.

Finally there came a lull, and Judge Cooley, a gray-haired, pleasant-faced gentleman, passed into the room where the lads were waiting to learn their fate.

Taking a seat in front of the little culprits, who were seated in a group looking very much frightened, the judge said: "Boys, this is a sad business. You have pleaded guilty to a crime the penalty for which is a term of years in the reform school. It is probably best that you be sentenced to that institution. If you are given your liberty it will only be to go from bad to worse, and you will finally commit some much graver crime. I am sorry for you. Your position is a sad one indeed."

Then to the youngest: "Do you want to see your mother before you go down?" The lips of the lad, who was a clean-faced, bright-eyed, curly-haired little fellow, quivered at the mention of his mother's name, and he could hardly control his voice to answer, "Yes, sir."

The same question was asked the second, a lad of 12, a trifle more stolid in appearance, but there was a tremor in the voice as he too answered earnestly in the affirmative.

"And you, my lad?" to the oldest, whose unkempt appearance must have prompted the question which followed. "Is your mother in the city?" "No, sir." "When will she be here?" "Tomorrow." "Where is your father?" "I don't know—in Milwaukee, I believe." "What is he doing?" "I don't know, sir." "Do you want to see your mother before you go down?" "Yes, sir."

The kindly face of Judge Cooley was very sober as he looked at this lad. "It is a sad case," he said in aside to Clerk Stevens, "and it will be a kindness to the boy to send him to the reform school, where he will have a home and care."

The lad has a history that is calculated to win for him the sympathy and pity of all but the most depraved. The father and mother separated years ago, the former apparently no longer takes interest in his child's welfare. The mother is a woman of bad character, "though," said Clerk Stevens to the reporter, "it can be said to her credit that she does her best to hide her misdeeds from the lad; but a

These Minneapolis boys knew how to stay out of trouble in 1881: they hawked copies of the *Minneapolis Journal. Courtesy of the Hennepin County Library, Minneapolis Collection.*

boy of his age sees enough and hears enough from his companions to know that all is not right."

"Boys," said the judge, who had been very attentively studying the faces of the two younger lads for some moments, "if I permit you to go home now, will you report here tomorrow morning at 9 o'clock to learn the final disposition of your cases?" Both little faces brightened and both quickly responded, "Yes, sir." "Can I trust you?" "Yes, sir." "Well, you can go." "Now?" "Yes." And they were off like a flash.

"Wait, my lad," said the judge to the oldest, who had started with the others, "you must stay with the officer until your mother comes. You are older than your companions, and appear to have been their leader in the commission of this crime. I shall send you to the reform school, but you shall first see your mother."

The boy resumed his seat, and for some minutes his sobs only broke the stillness. Judge Cooley looked sober. His duty was evidently a painful one. The court officers seemed moved by the peculiarly sad lot of a boy who had been deserted by his father and who was worse than motherless.

"I will talk a little farther with the younger lads in the morning," said the judge, "and suspend sentence. It is probably their first criminal act, and may be their last."

A CROWDED STEAMER CAPSIZES ON LAKE PEPIN

JULY 14, 1890, *MINNEAPOLIS TRIBUNE*

*P*owerful thunderstorms moved through Minnesota on a steamy Sunday afternoon in July 1890. A huge tornado, later immortalized in a Julius Holm painting, churned across Kohlman Lake, "a little summering place" in what is now Maplewood. At least seven people were killed and dozens injured.

That evening, about seventy miles to the southeast, on Lake Pepin, a much larger tragedy unfolded. A "cyclone" blew in from the west, capsizing a steamer carrying more than one hundred passengers and crew up the Mississippi River. A Tribune correspondent who happened to be on the scene told the tale in gripping—if maddeningly chronological—fashion:

DROWNED!
An Awful Disaster At Lake Pepin, Minn.
A Steamer Capsizes With 150 People Aboard.
The Wind and Waves Have no Mercy on Them.
Only Twenty Succeed in Saving Their Lives.
People Watch the Awful Struggle From the Shore.
But no One Could Lend Any Assistance.
The Storm Drowned the Cries of the Unfortunates.
A Disaster Never Before Equaled in the Northwest.

Lake City, Minn., July 13.—[Special.]—What may prove the most disastrous storm in many years passed over this place this evening killing probably 100 people and damaging property to an extent that at this writing cannot be estimated. Your correspondent was visiting friends in Lake City and was sitting in the yard when what appeared to be an ordinary electric storm was noticed coming up from the West. In

The Minneapolis Tribune.

VOL. XXIV., NO. 64.		MONDAY MORNING, JULY 14, 1890.			PRICE: FIVE CENTS.
ALL IN A NUTSHELL.	**JOHN C. FREMONT.**	**DROWNED !**		**HELL'S FURY**	
News of the Day Boiled Down for Hasty Perusal.	The Famous Old Veteran Dies Suddenly In New York City.	An Awful Disaster at Lake Pepin, Minn.		Outdone by the Elements at St. Paul.	
	An Attack of Peritonitis for Which Relief Came Not.	A Steamer Capsizes With 150 People Aboard.		A Tornado Whirls Across the Edge of the City.	
	He Was Out on Friday in Apparently Good				

One- and two-word headlines—DROWNED! and HELL'S FURY—were a fixture in the *Minneapolis Tribune* of the 1890s.

half an hour the whole heavens were converted into a complete canopy of lightning which was watched with interest by the brave citizens of the little village and with fear by the timid women and children. A little before dark a terrific wind struck the community and your reporter sought the shelter of the house just in time to escape being caught under a huge tree that came crashing down against the house. Windows were closed instantly and none too soon, for the cyclone was upon us and trees and houses were fast being demolished in its path.

While my wife, in fear and trembling, sought the seclusion and protection of the cellar in company with the ladies, I assisted in closing shutters and making preparations for the worst that could be expected while trees were heard to be crashing down and missiles were striking against the house. The building proved strong enough to weather the blast, and in half an hour the worst of the hurricane had passed. As soon as the trees had been cleared away from the front of the house your correspondent started out and soon learned

THAT A HORRIBLE CALAMITY

had befallen the place, that had not been equaled since the St. Cloud cyclone several years ago. People began to gather on the streets, and in a few moments the news was scattered abroad that an excursion boat with over 200 people on it was capsized in the middle of Lake Pepin. The boat proved to be the steamer *Sea Wing*, which came down the lake from Diamond Bluff, a small place about 17 miles north of here, on an excursion to the encampment of the First regiment, N.G.S.M., which is being held a mile below this city. The steamer started back on the homeward trip about 8 o'clock, and although there were signs of an approaching storm, it was not considered in any way serious, and no danger was anticipated. The boat was crowded to its fullest capacity, about

150 Men, Women and Children
from Red Wing and Diamond Bluff being on board, and about 50
people on a barge which was attached to the side of the steamer.
When about opposite Lake City the boat began to feel the effects
of the storm; but the officers kept on the way. The storm increased
as the boat continued up the lake. In 15 minutes it was at its height.
Nearing Central Point, about two miles above Lake City, the steamer
was at the mercy of the waves, which were now washing over the
boat, and all was confusion. The boat momentarily ran onto a bar
and the barge was cut loose, and the steamer again set adrift in the
lake. A number of those on the barge jumped and swam ashore. As
the barge also floated again into the deep water those on the barge
saw the steamer as it was carried helplessly out into the middle of
the lake, and as they were being tossed about on the raging waters,
they were horrified a moment later to see the steamer and its cargo
of 150 people

Precipitate into the Lake.
Those on the barge remained there until they were drifted nearer
the shore and they were all rescued or swam ashore. Among them
were two ladies who were brought to the beach by strong and ready
swimmers. There were about 50 in all that were on the barge.

The events that transpired on the steamer after it separated from
the barge are probably most clearly stated by those who were rescued
from it about half an hour ago. It is now 12 o'clock midnight. As
soon as the [storm] had begun to affect the progress of the boat,
Capt. Weathern [Wethern, actually] gave instructions to run the
boat into the Wisconsin shore but it was a too terrible force of wind
and wave. In five minutes more the waves began to wash into the
boat and fill its lower decks, and while hailstones as large as hen's
eggs came down on the heads of the poor helpless creatures which
were huddled together on the top, a huge wave struck the craft on the
side at the same moment that a terrific blast of wind, more horribly
forcible than the others, came up and carried the boat over, all of
the people on board; 150 or more were thrown into the water, some
being caught underneath and others thrown into the waves.

The boat turned bottom upwards and only about 25 people were
observed to be floating on the surface. These caught hold of the
boat and climbed upon the upturned bottom, those first securing
a position assisting the others. In 10 minutes more than 25 or so
who had obtained momentary safety on the boat could observe no

others of the boat crew or passengers floating on the surface of the continuing high sea of waves. Afterwards, however, as a flash of lightning lighted up the surface of the lake, the sight of an occasional white dress of a drowning woman or child was observable, but it was impossible for those who witnessed the horrible sight

TO LEND ANY AID.

Those remaining began calling for help from the shore as soon as the storm began to abate and in half an hour lights were observed flitting about on the pier at Lake City, opposite which point the upturned steamer had now been driven. Before help could reach them, however, the creatures who remained to tell the horrors of the night were again submitted to another battle with the elements, with no word of warning; and as they were just beginning to hope that they would be taken off by the citizens of Lake City, the boat again turned over, this on its side and again all of the 25 remaining souls were hurtled into the water. Of these several were drowned before they could be brought to the boat by those who succeeded in remaining afloat and again securing hold of the boat's side. As the men hung on to the railing, in danger each moment of being washed away by the waves, one man observed the forms of two women wedged in between a stationary seat and the boat's side, both pale in death, as the lightning gleams lit up their upturned faces. Another man saw

The *Sea Wing*'s owner and captain, David Wethern, lost his wife and youngest son in the disaster. *Courtesy of the Minnesota Historical Society.*

two little girls floating past him as he hung with desperate efforts to the steamer's side.

Half an hour after the passage of the storm your reporter went with others to the dock where the steamer *Ethel Howard* was anchored safe from the storm. It was presumed that the steamer would at once proceed to the rescue of the drowning, but when I asked the captain, Mr. Howard, if he was going out to the rescue, he replied that he was not going to run his boat away from the shore until the indication of another approaching storm had disappeared. He said also that he did not propose to run the risk of losing his boat in order to look for dead people out on the lake. Citizens of Lake City, who heard Captain Howard's remarks, were most severe in their denunciation of this position he assumed in the face of the statements made to him that every minute might mean the saving of a half dozen lives. Many talked of taking the boat away from him by force, but there were not enough to put the threat into execution, and other means of rescue were resorted to. In a few minutes a dozen or more rowboats were manned and put out from the shore. The upturned boat was at last discovered;

The Twenty or more Remaining People
clinging to the boat were rescued and brought to the shore, most of them being men who could swim.

Among those who are known to have been on board the steamer and who are undoubtedly drowned are: Two children of C.H. Reberick, Peter Goken, his wife, five children and hired girl, Fred Sebes, wife and daughter, Mrs. Capt. Wethern and her two children, F. Christ, Wm. Blaker and family of three, Mrs. Hempting and daughter, Gus Beckmark; a Miss Flyn, Bose Adams and Ira Fulton. A full list of the 150 passengers, which are pretty certain to have been drowned, is not obtainable at this writing. A large majority of them were women and children. Those being saved being nearly all strong men, who were able to swim, and cling to the boat, after it had capsized. On the return from the capsized boat with three or four people who had been rescued, one of the row boats encountered two floating bodies, each with a life preserver attached.

In Lake City the damage to property by the cyclone is great, although no fatalities have been reported. Collins Bros.' saw and planning mill is totally demolished. The roof of the opera house, owned by Mr. Hanisch, was carried away and the stores underneath more or less damaged by the rain and hail.

Up to this time, 1:30 a.m., 62 bodies have been found and laid out.

COPS BREAK UP A POKER GAME

FEBRUARY 19, 1895, *MINNEAPOLIS TRIBUNE*

*A*fter reading this detailed account of a police raid on an illegal card game, one wonders if a Tribune reporter was among the card players gathered in the "dingy little room" at the back of a cigar store on Washington Avenue.

Broke Up Their Game

An Afternoon Card Party Interrupted by the Police Blue-Coats Raid an Apartment in Rear of a Cigar Store at 211 Washington Avenue South, and Catch 11 Men Intently Watching the Fate of a Jack-Pot—A Player Who Held an Ace Full at the Time Is Sorely Disappointed at His Ill-Luck—Names Given by the Prisoners.

"This is unfair, officer. Here I have an ace full on fives, and there is nearly $50 at stake in this pot. I have lost heavily and you have ruined my hopes of getting back what money I dropped in this game."

The speaker was one of a party of 11 men engaged in a stud poker game, which, at the time of the interruption yesterday, was in progress in a dingy little room in the rear of R.L. Henshell's cigar store, 211 Washington avenue south. The play had been going on all afternoon, and the cashier's box showed that nearly $100 worth of chips were in circulation. The game had been played with a small limit during its early stage, but several good hands were dealt out shortly before 5 o'clock in the afternoon, and the pot swelled gradually as the interest of each player increased. It was a jack pot, and the man next to the dealer opened it for a dollar. Several stayed, but when it was learned that the little light haired man at the end of the table did not draw cards, all but a trio dropped out. One of these held three of a kind when the draw was completed, another two pair, and the third a straight. The latter did most of the betting, and the rest could not get their money in the pot fast enough. The man with the two pairs became frightened when the second raise was made, and said he guessed he'd call. His friend with three of a kind followed suit, but when it came to the little man at the end of the table, he put in the necessary amount to see the raise, and said he'd go them $10 better, but the words had hardly fallen from his lips ere the man with a fur overcoat carelessly leaned over the table and secured possession of the little box the cashier had been watching so closely.

The fur-coated man's presence had a magic effect upon the men seated around the table. For a minute they sat and stared at him with awe, as if at a loss to account for his sudden appearance. It was simple enough, though. He had been on that beat more than a day, and had got wind of the fact that a quiet poker game was being conducted in the rear of the store daily. Attention was all centered on the big pot in the middle of the table, and none of the players had heard him open the front door and noiselessly make his way to the rear apartment. Even when he entered the room he was not noticed, so interested were the men with their cards. Officer Dugan, for he was the intruder, stood watching the game fully three minutes before his presence was discovered. Little resistance was offered. The gamblers accepted the situation in a philosophical manner, with the exception of the little light haired man, who had counted on raking in the pot by the disclosure of his full hand. He was of the opinion that he had good grounds to kick on, but the blue coat claimed a hand in the pot, and it was a winner, too.

The party was politely informed that the patrol wagon was in waiting for them in front, and they marched in single file through the cigar store and out onto the sidewalk, where a crowd of several hundred people had gathered to see what was up. The outfit was hustled off to the Central police station, and the wagon returned for the table and chips. Sergt. Leonard, who had conducted the raid, appeared at the police station and entered a charge of gambling

Miles upriver and some years earlier, the loggers of Camden enjoyed a card game undisturbed by Minneapolis police. *Courtesy of the Hennepin County Library, Minneapolis Collection.*

against each of the men. R. Henshell, the proprietor of the place, was not arrested, but the sergeant stated that he would be brought into the police court today. The men arrested gave the names of Andrew Iverson, G. Anderson, C.M. Phillips, Charles Hanson, James Thompson, P. Mulley, James Miller, Charles Alberts, William Kline, Albert Manning, George Meghen.

BUGGY RAGE FLARES ON PORTLAND AVENUE

FEBRUARY 8, 1898, *MINNEAPOLIS TRIBUNE*

Four men—first one pair and then another—stepped out of their carriages one Sunday morning and, without a word, began whipping one another on Portland Avenue near Fifteenth Street. The Tribune *gave readers a blow-by-blow account of what might be the first reported incident of road rage in Minnesota:*

WAS FULL OF MYSTERY
MEN AND DOGS FALL OUT AND CHIDE AND FIGHT, CREATING A DIVERSION AND DISTURBING THE PEACE OF THE SABBATH ON PORTLAND AVENUE.

The peace and quiet of Portland avenue was ruthlessly disturbed Sunday morning. Two whip fights and a dog fight occurred on that ordinarily well behaved thoroughfare. It all happened so suddenly that the residents did not have time to find out the cause of the principals, and they have nothing but the recollection of the affair. It will, however, serve as a topic for neighborly gossip, and much speculation will be indulged in.

Just about the time the churches were letting out, two men in carriages approached one another from opposite directions. They met near Fifteenth street. Without a word they stopped their swiftly speeding horses, jumped out, grabbed their buggy whips and fought a furious round for about two minutes. Blows fell with lightning

Horses paused at a watering spot at the foot of the Hennepin Avenue bridge in downtown Minneapolis in the 1890s or early 1900s. *Courtesy of the Hennepin County Library, Minneapolis Collection.*

rapidity. Not a word was spoken, but standing about six feet apart they roundly slashed and struck at one another.

The old saying "like master, like man" was never more true than in this case. Each of the men was accompanied by a dog. One was a small bull-terrier. The other was a large dark brown St. Bernard. When they saw their masters having it out, they took a turn at fighting and chewed and bit each other until the big fellow obtained a good grip on the terrier's throat. Then it tried to sweep the streets with its adversary.

In the meantime the owner of the big dog had had his whip torn from his hand, and to save himself went into the fight at close quarters. He grabbed the other man by the shoulders, pushed him into the snow, and was showering bitter blows on the under man when bystanders took a hand.

As the fight was at its height, two more men drove up and went through the same operation. They took out their buggy whips and slashed each other across the face. However, their fight was tame compared to the first one.

Although the affair only lasted about two minutes, it gave a few bystanders a chance to congregate. When the four men had been separated, it was found that the dogs were still at it, and it required several good hard kicks to subdue the animals. Then without a word of explanation the men got into their buggies and drove away. What the cause of the feud was, or who the men were, is still a mystery to the few who witnessed it. The men had stylish turnouts and were well dressed and good looking.

THE PENNILESS PRIMA DONNA

DECEMBER 9, 1899, *MINNEAPOLIS TRIBUNE*

A century before Google and YouTube and Facebook, it was much easier for a person to erase the memory of a public humiliation and emerge years later as a respected professional in the very city in which the humiliation had been widely reported and discussed. Here, in stories published sixteen years apart, the Tribune *recounts the fall—and, perhaps, rise—of Lillian M. Knott.*

HER STORY PATHETIC
LILLIAN KNOTT, ONCE A PROMINENT AND TALENTED SINGER, NOW AT
A WASH TUB IN THE MINNEAPOLIS WORKHOUSE.
SHE RECITES THE SORROWFUL CAUSES AND CONDITIONS WHICH LED
TO HER DISGRACE AND DOWNFALL.

As she toiled at a washtub in the convicts' department at the work house yesterday, with tears running down her face and her attitude that of a person who has lost her last friend, it was hard to see in Lillian Murray Knott, serving sentence of 40 days imprisonment for the theft of a cloak from a colored woman, a once popular singer, who in her prime drew a salary of perhaps $300 per week.

The story of Miss Knott, or rather Mrs. Joseph Barnett, to call her by her legal name, is a pathetic one, and shows what sickness, misfortune and general ill-luck can do for a person when it tries, and when the victim fails to make a hard fight against the conditions which confront her. If Miss Knott were not a singer of national reputation, and if she had not a father of the highest respectability in Terre Haute, Ind., her case would be but one of hundreds of others, but as it is, it is decidedly out of the common.

Miss Knott was arrested several days ago on complaint of Minnie Steele, a colored woman, who accused her of having stolen from her a cloak. As the Knott woman was wearing the garment at the time of her arrest, and as her explanation of how it came into her possession did not accord with the strict notions of honesty entertained by the judge of the police court, Lillian was sent to the work house to serve out a sentence.

There are but few women on the stage today who are superior in singing ability to Miss Knott, yet in spite of this she has been working in a variety theater in this city, a pitifully small salary, in order to get money enough to take her to the home of her parents, where she was assured of a welcome. She claims she was on her way to the ticket office to get a ticket her father sent her when she was arrested, wearing the cloak which has caused all the trouble, and she insists the garment had been loaned to her by the colored woman.

STORY OF HER CAREER.

Miss Knott was born in Marietta, Ohio, and when a child developed such a taste for singing that she was given every advantage that money could purchase. She was a student for six years in the Cincinnati college of music, and completed her education in Boston, after her parents had removed to Terre Haute, where her father is the manager of the Wabash Iron works. After completing her studies in Boston Miss Knott began her professional career which has terminated in the Minneapolis work house.

She appeared first with the Duff Opera company, singing in the role of prima donna. Then for two years she was understudy for Camille D'Arville, and later sang leads for Corinne. Afterwards, when leading lady with the company of Joe Flynn, in "McGinty, the Sport," she was married to Mr. Barnett, who was musical director of the company. When in St. Paul, she says, her husband deserted her, and since then she has been making her own living.

For a long time she sang in the cheap variety theaters of the Twin Cities, trying to save enough money to take her home, and just when she had saved the desired sum she was taken ill and forced to give up her position. Then she had to go to the hospital, where she remained long enough to spend all of her money, and when she emerged she was weak and penniless, and without a friend in the city to whom she could turn for aid.

Several days ago Miss Knott wrote to her father, asking him to send her a ticket, and, according to her story, he did so, and the ticket is now at the office of the company awaiting her order. Speaking of her case Miss Knott says:

A BORN SINGER.

"I was born in Marietta. I loved singing from a little thing in short dresses. When I was old enough, my parents gave me the best vocal instruction the place afforded and afterwards sent me to the Cincinnati College of Music where I was a student for six years. Then I received final instruction of a Boston vocal school and made my first professional debut with the Duff Opera company, singing prima donna roles. After that I was understudy with Camille D'Arville for two years and then I sang leads with Corinne.

"Then I was induced by the promise of a good salary to go out with Joe Flynn as leading lady in a play called 'McGinty, the Sport.' It was while with that company that I married Mr. Barnett. He was the musical director of the company. We came to St. Paul together and I sang in music halls to get money enough to go East and try for another engagement. Mr. Barnett left me.

"I persisted in my music hall singing amid the most degrading surroundings, so that I could redeem myself and go home presenting a respectable appearance. Then came the typhoid fever and what little I had was dissipated in a week. After I got out of the hospital, I sang at the Palm Garden in St. Paul, but my strength was gone and I feared to go on the stage, because I thought I should fall over the footlights.

"It was in this extremity that I wrote to my father and told him I was in trouble. He promptly replied that he had sent me a ticket and money. I cannot do the work to which I have been assigned in this prison. I have but just recovered from typhoid fever and—and I have never done any washing before.

"I realize that this ends my career. Nothing can be done for me now. I am the consort of common criminals, and, according to the verdict of the court, a criminal myself, but the court erred. I am quite innocent. I didn't steal the coat. I didn't know the colored woman at all—never saw her in all my life before.

Trouble Over Names.

"I had been to the Milwaukee ticket office to see about my ticket from papa. They said the ticket had been ordered for me, but that it had been issued in the name of Lillian Knott, and, of course, my true name is Mrs. Barnett. Mr. Rogers, the ticket agent, told me the rules of the company would compel him to wire the head office and find out if he could issue the ticket to me as Mrs. Barnett.

"I was ill and disheartened and it was a very cold day. I had no cloak or winter garment of any sort. After coming out of the hospital I had nothing, positively nothing that a woman ought to have. I suppose it was because I was so broken-hearted that I went down to the Milwaukee depot and saw the train go out. I don't know what made me do it, except that I knew the train was homeward bound, and I just wanted to look at it—that was all.

"When I was coming out of the depot I met a colored man whom I had known as an attaché of a local variety theater. He always seemed to me a respectable man. He spoke to me and remarked that I was shivering. It was fearfully cold, and you see I hardly had any clothes on. He said his wife lived near by, and they had a fire, and he invited me to go there and get warm. I had to go somewhere. I was freezing.

"So I went to the place—where it was I do not know. When we entered it seemed to me the woman had been drinking. I had never seen her before. The colored people were very kind to me, and when I told them that I was going to the Milwaukee office to get my ticket for home, the woman offered to lend me her cloak to wear on the way.

Wanted a Kind Word.

"A short time after I borrowed the cloak I was arrested on the street for stealing it. Perhaps the woman really thought that I would get my ticket and leave for home with the cloak. It was a cloak upon which I would not have allowed my little dog to sleep three years ago, but I do not say that in a spirit of unthankfulness.

"I have found by bitter experience that white skins do not make kind hearts. The colored man seemed disposed to be kind to me.

An aerial view of the Minneapolis Workhouse in about 1900. *Courtesy of the Hennepin County Library, Minneapolis Collection.*

At the moment that I met him, had a dog licked my hand I would have fallen on my knees and embraced him. Do you know what it is to be ill and lonely and hungry and a stranger, to crave a civil word or a kindly smile where neither are to be had? I might have sold my soul for them—I had sold everything else—why not?

"At this place the officials are kind, but I really am not strong enough for such work, and, besides, my ticket to take me home is in Minneapolis, and I am sure there is money there for me, too. Why will they not let me go? I have done nothing to be sent here for. I am innocent of any offense except being ill and in want."

The next day, the Tribune *reported that Knott had been released from the workhouse and was on her way home to Terre Haute. A number of sympathetic Elks had raised forty dollars and paid her fine. Before her release, she met with the grand jury and repeated the story she had told the* Tribune, *describing with "graphic emphasis the details of the alleged theft" and denying "as firmly as ever" that she had stolen the garment.*

Several supporters materialized and appealed to the judge to drop the charge, but he was unmoved: "If the accusation were a true one, as I believe it was, this young woman has received no more than her just deserts. The testimony of the police is that she has been leading a dissolute life and been consorting with disreputable characters for some time."

That's the last we hear of the penniless prima donna. Or is it?

Sixteen years later, on September 19, 1915, the Tribune *trumpeted the appointment of one Lillian M. Knott as director of the public school music department of the Northwestern Conservatory in Minneapolis. This Knott had spent the previous five years at Tulane University in New Orleans, leading the school's "public school music department," and the previous ten summers directing a music program for Louisiana teachers.*

Could it be the same Miss Knott? The story doesn't mention a background in opera, let alone a workhouse stint. But it does note that she "received her musical education in the New England Conservatory," which matches the claim of the singer arrested in 1899. Is it possible that two women named Lillian M. Knott earned a music degree in the same city about the same time and later found work in Minneapolis? It seems unlikely.

TWENTY - FIVE YEARS BEHIND BARS

JULY 11, 1901, *MINNEAPOLIS TRIBUNE*

Cole and Jim Younger spent nearly twenty-five years in Minnesota's Stillwater prison for their part in the Jesse James gang's failed bank robbery in Northfield in 1876. A Tribune *reporter interviewed the brothers on the day their parole was granted. The Youngers discussed the development of the telephone and "Edison's talking machine," the march of slang and the effect of imprisonment on the human mind. They spoke thoughtfully and at length.*

Jim Younger, who said his optimistic outlook kept him sane during his long imprisonment, killed himself in St. Paul a year after his release, reportedly after a broken love affair. Cole Younger, who wrote a memoir, appeared in Wild West shows and later declared he had become a Christian, died in Missouri in 1916.

REJOICING
YOUNGER BROTHERS TELL THE TRIBUNE OF THEIR EXPERIENCES

A representative of The Tribune talked with the Youngers before their release was ordered. Both men expressed a desire to keep out of print now and for all future time. They have been talked to death in the newspapers, and many writers publishing alleged interviews did so without warrant.

The effect was prejudicial to their chance of release. To find a man boasting over the newspaper columns, between quotation marks of daring deeds he did in old guerilla days, is to create suspicion that he still has a soft spot in his heart for the old adventurous life,

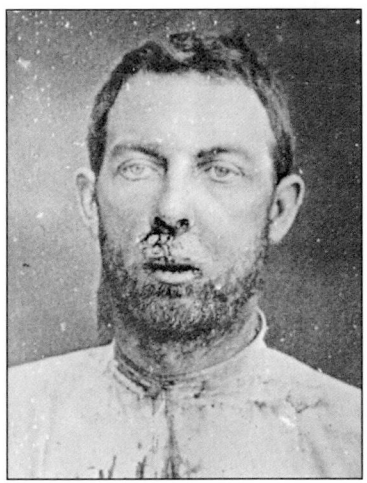 

Jim Younger (left) and brother Cole looked like beaten men shortly after their capture in 1876.

but when it is found that the man quoted never uttered any of the statements attributed to him—that the whole story as published was pure invention—the injustice may be understood.

Warden Wolfer strives the keynote of the situation when he asserts that sustained public interest, conflicting public opinion concerning the Youngers has been due to the insistence of newspaper editors on making copy about the men. In many cases articles written have been largely imaginative, and utterances of the prisoners have been made to serve as the basis for unfair deduction. Not long ago a writer for a St. Louis newspaper interviewed the men and when his article was read in the prison it proved as fanciful as any of Grim's fairy tales.

"When I get outside the prison door, if ever I do get out," said Cole Younger yesterday, "I believe there is agility enough in my old bones to let me turn just one somersault. I feel like a 10-year-old boy at the mere possibility. Beyond any doubt the actuality will overcome me to the extent of just one old-fashioned handspring."

"Me, too," interrupted Jim. "Remember the time they let us go over on the wall to the warden's house that time—must be eight years ago?"

EFFECT OF LONG IMPRISONMENT.

"I can remember the way everything looked, right now," said Cole. "It's very strange," he went on reflectively—"the effect that long confinement produces on one's ideas of space. I don't quite know whether the muscles of the eyes contract, or whether it is refusal of the brain to immediately comprehend what the eyes see, but when a man has been in close confinement between walls for so long a time he doesn't seem able to grasp the ideas of distance. I remember staring over at the Wisconsin hills that were all green and beautiful. I wanted to stay there until I could get used to the sensation, but of course couldn't.

"'How does that make you feel,' I asked my brother.

"'Feel as if I were about to fall off something high,' he said.

"But of course that will soon wear off. I want to get out of this prison because I have reached the limit of my capacity for taking punishment. We have been kindly and well treated, according to our merits as prisoners, but you people who live on the outside and talk so glibly of life imprisonment—why, not one of you has any conception of its meaning.

"It is burial without death. Only by exercising his will power in a systematic and never-ceasing struggle with the melancholy born of solitude, can a man evade insanity. I don't mean violent, straight-jacket insanity, perhaps though some might come to that, but the dreadful haunting dread of mental failure suggested by introspection.

"I know nothing of mental science except such things as I have read while in jail, without the power to properly digest them, but it seems to me that this fear of becoming insane and the constant strain of trying not to is really the most torturing form of insanity.

"It may be functional, as the doctors say, and not organic, but unless the will of the sufferer is tremendously strong he endures the tortures of the damned."

DATES FROM THE FIRE.

"Have you never been outside but that once?" was asked.

"Yes—the night of the fire. Everything modern dates from the night of the fire.

"If we are paroled," said Jim Younger, "we shall get in a quiet corner somewhere, so that the sights and sounds of the world will be visible and audible, but we have no desire to do aught else than labor quietly to the end of our days. This will afford us the opportunity we have been seeking for a long time—that of showing the world that we know how to live decently and honestly and hold trustworthy positions as men among men.

"I don't think I shall be much disturbed by the mechanical and engineering advances that have occurred in the last 25 years," said Jim, reflectively. "You see engineering is my hobby. I take the *Scientific American* and have had it for many years. Every issue of that paper I have studied carefully. When the first electrical cars were put in use I saw the cuts and wrestled with them and the descriptions given until I understood the principle. Now, of course, it will look odd to see a carriage running round without horses, or a big car traveling without mules or steam, but for years I have known that these things were, and pictures have familiarized me with their appearance. It will all be novel—very new and novel, but not incomprehensible."

USED A TELEPHONE.

"Well," remarked Cole, "the telephone and Edison's talking machines have always been my limit. Once when I was down in the office I had orders to telephone over to the warden's house. That tickled me to death, because I had heard them talking at one end of the line, and it was all I could do to keep my face straight at the spectacle of a fellow jabbering into a dumbbell—'wha-a-t!—yes—did he?—who said so!—all right—tell him to come down this afternoon.'

"I heard that and never forgot it. When they showed me how to ring for the warden I put my ear to the thing and waited. When the warden said 'hello' at the other end of that line it sounded so close at hand, and the whole thing seemed so absurdly impossible that I was rattled. I couldn't reply for a minute or more.

"Now they have lines from Minneapolis to New York, and you can talk just as easily as to the warden's house," said Jim, out of his superior knowledge.

"I heard about it," replied Cole, "when I have a chance I'm going to try that if it costs a dollar."

"To the man who has been in prison so long as I have," said Jim, "access to all the modern books and magazines is a blessing not unmixed with pain. You see, every magazine story, every novel, every scientific treatise, everything printed, in fact, contains references to events and things in common, everyday use of which the prison

After his release, Cole Younger toured the country in a Wild West show. *Courtesy of the Library of Congress.*

reader comprehends nothing. He reads half-comprehendingly, and longs and longs for freedom, if only for a little time, that he may once more get in tune with the world and be at least able to read of it intelligently. Still, the man in prison who reads, must, I think, be held a good critic on some matters. Take the modern march of slang, for instance.

THE MARCH OF SLANG.

"I have noticed that a slang word appears first, perhaps, in a publication of the lower class. It has probably been accepted by certain classes of people before it reaches the papers at all. Now, here in the solitude of the prison library, I watch the evolution of that slang word. It crawls insidiously from the newspaper to the cheaper magazine, where it appears most likely in a story of the day. In a subsequent issue the editor of the magazine uses it editorially to express some idea. Next month I discover it in one of the heavier publications, quoted, most likely, but still there. From that time the position of the word is assured, because writers of ponderous leaders on electrical engineering in the *Electrical Magazine* are not without their weaknesses, and they, too, pick the word up.

"For people outside, the setting of such words as I refer to in conversation may remove the impression of their absurdity, but to a man in jail, with nothing but books to talk to, some of these phrases sound like infant babbling. And to tell the truth, great as my opportunities have been for reading of late years, I still tie to Dickens. He doesn't clip his English, he doesn't slang it, and his writings are full of heartbeats. I have laughed with him and wept with him. Great is Dickens."

"Do you mean to say, you two, that the confinement here really made you fear insanity?"

MEN AFRAID OF THEMSELVES.

"God knows what it is that men fear who are shut up for life," said the librarian. "I think it is that a man becomes afraid of himself—doubtful of his ability to sustain the awful routine of life under restraint. It is not the prison that hurts—it is a splendid institution. A well behaved man can live here in entire physical comfort, but the human mind requires a wider range of activity than that possible behind stone walls. The prisoner who desires to live out his sentence without mental deterioration must develop mental activities thought of outside a place like this.

"For many years I have never permitted myself to harbor a bad thought about anyone. Mind, I do not say I have not had such thoughts. They flash into one's mind and would take root and grow there if not at once cast out. My method has been, when so assailed by my evil genius, to deliberately force a train of thought on another and more pleasant subject. It is hard to do, but it can be done.

Stillwater Prison in its winter finery, in about 1900. *Courtesy of the Minnesota Historical Society.*

"A long time ago, down in Missouri, I knew an old lady about 70 years old, whose husband was about 80, I should think. People used to say that in all their married life those two had never been angry at each other, nor uttered a cross word. One day I asked the old lady how that was.

"'James,' she said, 'when I married my mother said to me that I was marrying a man and not an angel. She warned me that if I desired to lead a happy life I must look always for the good in my husband and shut my eyes to the bad. Now, I have seen great good in him—I have never seen any bad, and we have never quarreled.'

"I believe in that old lady's philosophy," said Jim, "and I have looked for the brighter side of things ever since coming in here, otherwise I should have died long ago, a mania most likely. Both Cole and I have cultivated control until I think either of us could command our feelings in the most awful situation conceivable. Perhaps you can conceive that situation."

ICE YACHT REDUCED TO KINDLING

MARCH 2, 1903, *MINNEAPOLIS TRIBUNE*

*M*ore than a century ago, well-heeled winter sailors began plying the surface of Lake Minnetonka in ice yachts. The large wooden craft, some more than thirty feet long and capable of carrying eight people, were fitted with sails and iron-shod runners. The new sport satisfied a pre-snowmobile appetite for winter thrills, with daredevil turns and speeds topping forty miles per hour.

Danger was part of the thrill, and death, injury and narrow escapes were the stuff of breathless newspaper stories. In December 1907, an eleven-year-old girl was killed by a speeding iceboat on Lake Calhoun. In February 1908, an eighteen-year-old woman suffered a skull fracture when two boats collided in the dark on Calhoun. And later that month, a boy strapped to the seat of his boat sailed into open water on the same lake; another sailor pulled the submerged boy—and the boat—to safety.

Some accidents were more amusing than tragic. One unfortunately named sailor, Commodore Wetmore, forgot to anchor his unattended vessel on a windy day on Lake Minnetonka. The account of his ill-fated outing landed on page three of the Tribune:

Is Kindling Wood
Awful Fate Befalls Theo. Wetmore's Ice Yacht.
Handsome and Speedy Minnetonka Craft Goes Searching for a
Race Minus the Commodore, and Ends Up by Crashing Into a
Pile at the Blue Line Pavilion—Jaunty Suit of Blue Discarded,
and His Sailor's Cap Has Been Hung on the Wall.

The Minnetonka Ice Yacht Club opened on St. Louis Bay in 1900. The 167-member club commanded more than thirty-five vessels, some shipped in from the East Coast. *Courtesy of the Hennepin County Library, Minneapolis Collection.*

Yesterday Commodore Wetmore, of the Minnetonka Ice Yacht club, had a beautiful and speedy ice boat which was not only the pride of the commodore's heart, but also the envy of all the ice boaters of the Minnetonka club. Today the commodore is without his boat, and his rank as commanding officer of the ice fleet seems to him nothing but the merest mockery and deceit.

He still commands, and still has all of the jauntiness of the true salt that he is, but his walk has lost some of its swagger, and his nautical commands have become but low whispers heard only by the passing breeze. The jaunty suit of blue has been discarded, and the sailor's cap has been hung on the wall. Forgotten are the "shiver my timbers," and "blast my topsail." The hands that but yesterday knew the tiller and main sheet will soon lose their cunning learned by years and months of toil on the freshwater sea, and the voice that was wont to command in tones of thunder will not again this winter be heard to even whistle for a breeze.

Yesterday the commodore with three friends started for a sail in his fine ice yacht, the *North Star*. A spanking breeze was blowing that sent the boat along at a forty-knot clip, and the speedy clipper seemed to scarcely touch the ice as she sped with the wings of a bird up the lake. Pride and joy were in the commodore's heart as he went speeding over the ice, secure in the thought that there was no boat on the lake that could show him a clean pair of heels, and only one that could even give him a good race. This boat he was looking for, and it was Commodore Sampson's *Red Dragon* at Excelsior.

Now Commodore Wetmore was bent up the lake with the solo hope that he might meet this same *Red Dragon* and settle once and for all the superiority of his craft. So he proudly and boastfully sailed up and down along the water front of Excelsior, flaunting his battle pennant to the breeze as a challenge to any who might wish to try their mettle.

The *North Star* sailed back and forth, but no reply came to the silent challenge, the Excelsior boats being somewhat daunted by the bold defiant air of the gruff old sea dog, who so dared to beard them in their den. Finally Commodore Wetmore and his friends stopped the boat and stood on the ice discussing their contempt of anything that had sails on that part of the lake. In the heat of their imprecations they forgot that they had not moored the *North Star*, and suddenly the sails of the boat filled with an extra heavy gale, and the boat started in a mad chase across the bay.

Any attempts to stop the boat were useless as it was off with the speed of the wind, and almost before the commodore realized that his craft had started for parts unknown, it had bumped into one of the piles at the Blue Line pavilion. The beautiful boat was smashed into kindling wood, and the proud pennant of the commodore was thrown with the violence of the gale to a cold resting place on the ice.

A team of horses was obtained, and the wreck of the late ice challenger was hauled ruefully homeward. The sturdy commodore also took the vehicle and went home by a somewhat slower method, and more roundabout way than he had come.

ST. PAUL'S FIRST ROAD FATALITY

MAY 29, 1903, *MINNEAPOLIS TRIBUNE*

*E*ight-year-old Irene Max was the first person killed by an automobile in St. Paul. The story of her tragic end made the front page of the Tribune. It's a dramatic account, rich with detail and good quotes but marred by significant errors. The victim's first name, for example, is reported incorrectly as Arania.

At the wheel that evening was Horace H. Irvine, the son of lumberman Thomas Irvine. Horace Irvine, twenty-five, was one of a handful of St. Paulites with the means to afford an automobile that cost more than $60,000 in today's currency.

Irvine was already making his mark as a partner in his father's business and was a director of the Weyerhaeuser Timber Company. A few years after the accident, he married Clotilde McCullough. The couple built a fourteen-thousand-square-foot mansion at 1006 Summit Avenue, where they raised their four children. The two youngest daughters, Coco and Olivia, donated the mansion—now in use as the Governor's Residence—to the State of Minnesota in 1965.

CHILD KILLED BY AN AUTO
ARANIA MAX OF ST. PAUL, AGED 8,
STRUCK DOWN BY H. IRVINE'S MACHINE
SHE DIES INSTANTLY
CHAUFFEUR BLOWS HORN REPEATEDLY BUT
CHILD IS CONFUSED BY CAR
HE GOES TO STATION
IS RELEASED TILL THIS MORNING—WOMEN SWOON AND
MOTHER IS HYSTERICAL

Arania Max, the eight-year-old daughter of Peter Max, 661 Hague Avenue, St. Paul, was run down by an automobile at St. Albans street and Selby avenue last evening and instantly killed.

The chaffeur was Horace Irvine, son of Thomas Irvine of 673 Dayton avenue, and in the automobile with him were William Ernst and Miss Allen and Miss Fitzpatrick. The little girl's death was caused by a fracture at the base of the skull.

Mr. Irwin had recently purchased the automobile at a cost of $2,500 and last evening invited his friends for a ride.

They had not been out long when they drove down Selby avenue after a spin on Summit avenue and other streets on the hill.

Witnesses say that the automobile with its aristocratic occupants drove several times up and down Selby avenue on that portion of the street paved with asphalt and at one time had a brush with a machine of lesser proportions.

Confused by Car.

Mr. Irvine was sitting proudly with both hands on the steering apparatus when St. Albans street was approached. Two little girls, Arania Max and Sadie Mundt, of the same age, were seen playing in the street just below St. Albans.

One of the girls was on the sidewalk while the Max girl was on the street car tracks. As the ponderous vehicle was approaching them the Mundt girl called to her companion.

"Come back, Arania, here comes the automobile!"

A street car was approaching at the same time and the Max child stood in the center of the street somewhat bewildered and then started to dash back again to her playmate. The chaffeur steered his machine close to the curb in an effort to avert an accident and again tooted the horn a couple of times.

It was too late.

The little girl raised her hands above her head and at the same instant she was struck in the right side by the body of the automobile.

She fell face downwards on the pavement and broke her neck, while the vehicle passed over her body and crossed to the opposite side of the street to avoid a second collision with a street car.

Mr. Irvine immediately stopped the vehicle and returned to where the corpse of the child lay in the street in a pool of blood that oozed from her mouth.

The sight shocked the ladies in the automobile, and Miss Allen swooned before she could be assisted to the ground by Willie Ernst. Mr. Irvine was overcome by the sight and stood motionless in the street.

Arania gazed at him, gave one gasp and expired just as Dr. A.P. Kearn reached the scene two minutes later.

MOTHER HYSTERICAL.

The body of the child was gently lifted from the street and rested on the green sward that skirts the sidewalk. Shortly afterwards a weeping mother came and became hysterical as her dead daughter was being bourne to the home, followed by several hundred people who had gathered quickly after the distressing accident.

Mr. Irvine and Mr. Ernest went to the Central police station and informed Capt. Hanft of the accident. They were detained at police headquarters for some time, while an effort was being made to locate County Attorney Kane, who was to decide what course should be pursued in regard to the chaffeur and his companion. Mr. Kane could not be found, and it was finally decided to allow the young men to return to their homes on condition that they report at the station this morning.

MR. IRVINE DISTRESSED.

Mr. Irvine, when asked about the accident, stated that he was so much distressed by the accident that he could not explain the affair very well.

"It was purely accidental," he said. "I blew the horn at the street crossing and twice again when I was approaching the children. I do not know which part of the machine struck her first.

"I tried my best to avoid the accident, but the little girl ran right in front of me, became bewildered, tried to turn back and fell in front of the vehicle. The wheels of the machine passed over the girl's body. I do not know exactly what speed I was going."

Willie Ernst said that he would not state the rate of speed at which the machine was going because he did not know. He said that he did not think it was very fast.

SADIE TELLS OF DEATH.

Sadie Mundt, the 9-year-old companion of the Max girl, who lives with her parents at 656 Selby avenue, said in regard to the accident:

The Wilcox Motor Company built automobiles at a plant at Tenth and Marshall Streets in northeast Minneapolis in the early 1900s. Here, one of the owners, John F. Wilcox, was out for a spin with his wife and three other passengers. *Courtesy of the Hennepin County Library, Minneapolis Collection.*

"We were playing wood tag. Arania ran into the street away from me. I saw the automobile coming and I shouted:

"'Arania, come back. See the automobile!'

"It wasn't going fast. Just like a street car. Arania ran towards me and she was knocked down by the wagon just near the sidewalk."

E.J. Sullivan, who was sitting outside his store, 676 Selby avenue, where the accident occurred, corroborates the story of the Mundt girl. He says that after running into the middle of the street that she was called back by her playmate and was caught before she reached the curb and mowed down.

Within days, the coroner investigating the case cleared Irvine of blame, ruling that the girl had darted in front of his automobile, which was traveling at no more than seven miles per hour. Irvine "felt so bad," the Tribune *reported on June 6, "that he was willing to do anything within reason that the parents suggested." In the end, he gave the girl's father $5,000 in cash to cover funeral costs and "prevent any further notoriety or danger of damage suits."*

MINNESOTA'S LAST EXECUTION

FEBRUARY 13, 1906, *ST. PAUL DAILY NEWS*

*I*n May 1905, itinerant worker William Williams was convicted of killing a St. Paul teen and the boy's mother and was sentenced to die by hanging. An 1889 state law designed to prevent executions from becoming public spectacles prohibited newspaper reporters from attending them and limited the number of witnesses to a few dozen. But a St. Paul Daily News reporter somehow managed to enter the basement of the Ramsey County Jail and write this dramatic and detailed account of the last execution to take place in Minnesota.

Reports of the Cornish immigrant's agonizing death eroded support for capital punishment in Minnesota, and the state abolished the death penalty in 1911.

THIS IS MURDER; I AM INNOCENT.
—WILLIAM WILLIAMS
SLAYER OF JOHNNY KELLER MAKES STATEMENT BEFORE BEING
STRANGLED TO DEATH

WAS RESIGNED TO HIS FATE.
"Gentlemen, you are witnessing an illegal hanging. This is a legal murder. I am accused of killing Johnny Keller. He was the best friend I ever had, and I hope to meet him in the other world. I never had improper relations with him. I am resigned to my fate. Goodbye."— William Williams' Last Words on Earth.

William Williams has been hanged.

The drop fell at 12:32 and he was cut down at 12:46, two minutes after physicians pronounced him dead.

Williams strangled to death.

His neck was not broken by the fall.

His feet touched the ground by reason of the fact that his neck stretched four and one-half inches and the rope nearly eight inches.

Deputies then pulled the rope so that Williams' head was kept up and strangulation could slowly go on. His feet touched ground all of the time that the death agonies were playing in his mind.

Slowly but surely life was squeezed from the body until at 12:46, just 14 minutes after the trap was sprung and 21½ minutes after Williams left his cell, death relieved the murderer of his suffering.

By JOSEPH E. HENNESSEY
THE ONLY NEWSPAPER MAN WHO WITNESSED THE EXECUTION

William Williams was strangled to death by three deputies holding the rope, which stretched, at 12:42 this morning in the basement of the county jail.

The execution was witnessed by 32 persons, all that the law allows.

Williams, who was the coolest man in the crowd, left his cell, accompanied by Father Cushen, at exactly 12:27. He walked to the elevator and then down the long flight of steps, smiling and chatting pleasantly with the priest and his two guards.

A photo of the gallows appeared in the *Minneapolis Tribune* the next day.

FACES ENGINE OF DEATH.

At the foot of the stairs Williams entered the death chamber and there before him stood the machine of execution.

Without uttering a word, but slightly pale, Williams, with long strides, reached the foot of the steps. Without hesitation he walked manfully and bravely up the steps and stood facing the crowd below.

Father Cushen stood beside the condemned man and the sheriff asked him if he had anything to say. With his hands handcuffed behind him, Williams faced his hearers, and with a firm voice, but slightly pale of face, spoke the words quoted above.

When he had finished the rope was placed around his neck and the black cap adjusted. In an instant Sheriff Miesen pulled the trap and the condemned man shot down.

TRAP IS SPRUNG.

The trap was sprung at exactly 12:32.

Gradually the rope stretched until the murderer's feet touched the floor. Then Deputies Frank Robert, Frank Picha and Frank Hanson took turns at holding up the body.

For 14 minutes the body hung there, Sheriff Miesen himself assisting at 12:44, when Williams was pronounced dead by the four physicians, Drs. Whitcomb, Miller, Ohage and Moore.

"Bill" Williams has paid the penalty of his crime.

No gamer man has walked to the scaffold in Minnesota.

With a smile on his lips, he joked with death.

With firm tread he descended to the sub-basement of the jail, where the scaffold awaited him.

It was just 12:22 when Sheriff Miesen entered Williams' cell and announced that the hour of death had come.

For an hour Father Cushen of the cathedral, who had converted Williams to the Catholic faith, had prayed with him.

Williams stood erect and said not a word.

Frank Robert, chief deputy, stood behind. Deputies Hanson and Picha handcuffed his hands behind his back.

The procession of death started. Williams walked alone. With firm tread he covered the 30 feet that lead to the elevator.

PRIEST AT ELBOW.

With the priest at his elbow, the deputies close at hand, he descended to the basement floor.

Then came the most trying ordeal of all. Williams, undaunted, started down the 27 steep iron steps that led to the sub-basement and death. Father Cushen hurried forward and clasped his arm about the murderer's shoulder. The deputies dropped behind.

Slowly the procession wound its way.

The door that reached to the large room beneath the cell house was reached. The door was opened. Electric lights cast a flood of bright rays on the prisoner.

A new spirit seemed instilled in Williams. He was to die as he had lived, caring naught for the future though death lurked only a score of feet away.

He rounded the ventilating fans of the jail.

Before him loomed the scaffold, grim striking, of yellow-tinted pine.

WILLIAMS QUIVERED.

For just a second Williams quivered. Then he looked death in the face and smiled.

"Hurry up," he whispered to Sheriff Miesen, and lengthened his steps.

Almost with a bound he was at the 13 steps that led to the scaffold platform and mounted eagerly.

The courthouse clock was striking 12:30.

From across the way the strains of music from a dance at Elks' hall penetrated softly, soothingly, to the inner recess of the jail.

"I am ready to die," murmured Williams.

Deputies aided him to the trap.

There was a sudden movement. Chief Deputy Robert had adjusted the black cap. Sheriff Miesen took a deep breath. He cast one glance toward Deputy Robert. Then his right hand grasped the fatal lever.

Click. Then a faint thud, and "Bill" Williams' body had dropped six full feet, and with a sudden jerk bounded upward.

BODY SWAYED.

Then it hung, swaying slightly from side to side. It was a twisted hemp rope that held the body that gripping tight about the throat was strangling the murderer of little Johnny Keller to death.

And, strange to say, the body did not whirl as is usually the case.

The black capped face still faced the audience. The body hung almost as it had stood upon the scaffold. The fingers scarcely twitched.

The legs did not contract.

"Bill" Williams, nervy, desperate, caring naught for life, was dying. The few spectators bared their heads. They stood transfixed with awe. It was the moment of death.

Not a sound was heard. Dr. George R. Moore, police surgeon, stepped forward and felt the dying man's pulse.

Drs. C.A. Wheaton and Justus Ohage stepped forward.

Then silence reigned.

Tick, tick, slowly the watch told the time.

Tick, tick—"Bill" Williams' soul was speeding to the great unknown that no man can fathom.

Five minutes, 10 minutes, 12 minutes, 14 minutes.

Still the spectators waited hushed with awe. The doctors' fingers were on "Bill" Williams' pulse.

Thirty seconds more.

"The man is dead," said Police Surgeon Moore. The other physicians nodded.

Deputy Frank Robert cut the rope.

"Bill" Williams, murderer of Johnny Keller, had paid the penalty of his crime.

The stark form was hurried to an undertaker's wagon and taken to the county morgue.

INDIFFERENT TO DEATH.

Yet this strange, incongruous "Bill" Williams was indifferent to death.

It was just 9 o'clock when his attorney, James Cormican, entered the jail, all hope gone.

"Billy," he said, "the jig is up."

"Won't the governor do something? Won't the British consul do something?" queried Williams.

Then Attorney Cormican recounted his effort of the afternoon. How he had been unable to stay the certain death of the gallows; how he had pleaded with Judge Lochren as Mrs. Lochren, with tears in her eyes, asked that the condemned man be given a chance for life. But the law is just and certain.

And Judge Lochren, despite his tender heart, heeds ever its mandates.

So there was naught he could do to stay the execution.

NOT AFRAID OF DEATH.

"What's the difference? I ain't afraid of death," said Williams. "I had 18 teeth pulled once and I think that is more pain than death will be."

Then Attorney Cormican gave him a paper which gave Williams' body to Mr. Cormican, but provides that the body must be interred in consecrated ground.

Williams signed the paper without hesitation.

"I don't want the doctors to cut me up," he said, "and send me around the world. They can cut my head up and take my brain—show people I am not crazy, that is all."

Attorney Cormican can claim the body any time within the next 36 hours, if he inters it in consecrated ground, and he can let the doctors make an examination of Williams' brain, if he wishes.

But Attorney Cormican would not see Williams die.

"Come and see my finish," urged Williams.

The basement of the Ramsey County Jail, shown here in about 1905, was the site of Minnesota's last execution. *Courtesy of the Minnesota Historical Society.*

"No, I can't, Bill," said Cormican. "I've done all I can for you. I don't want to see you die."

So at Mr. Cormican's request Williams named L.C. Cole to see him die, and John H. Hilger, who had been his death watch, and Rube Reynolds, a friend of Johnny Keller's, for whose death Williams had undergone the death penalty.

Then the attorney left.

Father Cushen, the man who had converted Williams, came.

It was not with hope of earthly life. It was the soul of Williams that he comforted. Yet, perhaps, more than anyone else, Father Cushen was responsible for Williams' calm demeanor, and for his strange indifference to death.

HE LOVED THE PRIEST.

"If I had met a man like that," Williams told his jailer, "I should not be in a murderer's cell now. I would have been an honest, upright, industrious man. I wish I had known him sooner. He is the only person besides Johnny Keller that seemed to care what became of me."

So Williams listened while Father Cushen prayed the last prayer for his soul.

So, devoutly the murderer knelt as the priest anointed his neck and head with sacred oil and pronounced the benediction.

Then "Bill" Williams rose from his knees ready to answer the summons of death.

Then he walked steadfastly to the scaffold, for he had learned to know the God that was a stranger to his youth.

KILLER WORE JEWELS IN JAIL

MARCH 18, 1910, *MINNEAPOLIS MORNING TRIBUNE*

Shades of Martha Stewart: Mrs. Lina Dale, a Minneapolis hotel proprietor charged with first-degree murder, managed to show a little style and grace behind bars, wearing jewels and volunteering to help with the laundry. Alas, no photos of her glittering form at the ironing board can be found.

Dale, whose first name was reported as Lena in other newspaper accounts, landed in the county jail after admitting to police that she had shot a man named William Lear during an argument. She said the shooting was accidental; she brandished the gun only to avoid another physical confrontation with a man who appears to have been her lover and tormentor.

After a brief trial the following month, a jury found her not guilty. The Morning Tribune *reported that she embraced and kissed each of the jurors after hearing the verdict "and then took an affectionate farewell with the matron of the county jail."*

DIAMOND-BEDECKED WOMAN WORKING IN JAIL LAUNDRY

With diamond earrings in her ears and rings on her fingers, Mrs. Lina Dale, who shot and killed William Lear several weeks ago in a fight at the Alberta hotel, 622 Hennepin avenue, is working in the laundry at the county jail while awaiting trial on a charge of murder.

The woman, who has retained her jewelry, although forced to don the jail uniform, spends three hours a day over the ironing board. The work is not compulsory, but it is preferred by the prisoner rather than spend the hours in idleness in her cell.

A THREE-YEAR-OLD STOPS TRAFFIC

SEPTEMBER 16, 1913, *MINNEAPOLIS MORNING TRIBUNE*

*T*his *delightful piece from the early days of the automobile appeared on page ten of* the Morning Tribune:

BABY AND HIS CART PUTS TRAFFIC IN MAZE
THREE-YEAR-OLD BOY IN MIDDLE OF STREET AT SEVENTH AND HENNEPIN.
EVERYBODY BUT THE POLICEMAN SEES HIM,
AND THERE'S A REASON FOR THAT.
WAIF SO SMALL THE TRAFFIC MAN ALMOST STEPPED ON HIM UNAWARES.

A little 3-year-old boy, with a two-wheeled cart with red and black trimmings, held up traffic at Seventh street and Hennepin avenue yesterday, and tied up street cars and switched automobiles into a double line that couldn't get past the corner.

Then he was taken up by the traffic policeman, turned over to another and turned loose in the corridor of the Central station jail, where he played horse with his cart, running up and down the tiled floor to the encouraging cheers of a score of prisoners waiting to be taken to the workhouse.

When they left to go up the river they waved farewells to the child.

ALMOST STEPPED ON HIM.
Patrolman Murray, stationed at Seventh street and Hennepin avenue, had blown his whistle for two automobiles to go out Hennepin

A busy stretch of Seventh Street between Marquette and Hennepin Avenues would have been a hazardous spot to leave a three-year-old unattended. *Courtesy of the Hennepin County Library, Minneapolis Collection.*

avenue. The automobilists started, then stopped. Murray beckoned impatiently to them and called to them to hurry. He blew his whistle. The autos didn't move an inch. A street car stopped.

Murray couldn't understand why they stopped. He blew on his whistle for the traffic on Seventh street to pass. It started. One auto got across. The next got half way and stuck in a line of wagons, street cars and autos. The policeman's whistle blew again and again.

"Say, untangle this mess and get that kid away," shouted one autoist to Murray, backing out to the line.

"What kid?" asked the policeman.

"The one behind you."

THERE WAS THE CAUSE.
Murray turned. A brown-eyed boy in blue rompers and a red sweater stood behind him right in the street where a street car passes every 45 seconds and scores of autos weave in and out.

Murray picked him up in his arms, took hold of the cart and went to the curbing. He put the boy down and told him to wait for him. He went back to the corner and untangled the lines of traffic and sent them on their way. Patrolman Brennan appeared. Murray took him over to the boy. Brennan took him to the police matron.

J. Skall, who manages a store at 110 Hennepin avenue, claimed the boy as his son yesterday afternoon. He said the lad had run away from the store wheeling the cart.

FLU OUTBREAK CLOSES CHURCHES, SCHOOLS, THEATERS

OCTOBER 13, 1918, *MINNEAPOLIS MORNING TRIBUNE*

*C*arried around the globe by massive troop movements at the end of World War I, Spanish influenza infected nearly half the world's population and killed more than twenty million people. In October 1918, word of the flu's growing presence in Minnesota began appearing on the front page of the Morning Tribune, below the news from the battlefields of Europe:

"Influenza Spread Held Slight Here"—October 2
"Epidemic in City Shows Slight Gain"—October 3
"Influenza Halts 'U' Opening…"—October 5
"8 Deaths From Influenza Here"—October 8
"Influenza Gains Slowly in City"—October 10
"Doctors Propose Drastic Lid Be Clamped on City"—October 11

By October 12, hundreds of new cases and a dozen or so deaths were being reported in Minneapolis each day. The city's health commissioner ordered all churches, schools, dance halls and theaters closed, beginning Sunday, October 13.

In the end, the flu killed 650,000 Americans, more than 10,000 in Minnesota. And as if war and pestilence weren't enough for Minnesotans to bear, fires smoldering near Bemidji and Brainerd were about to explode and race east, making October 1918 perhaps the ugliest month in state history.

INFLUENZA LID CLAMPED TIGHT ALL OVER CITY
NO CHURCH SERVICES TO BE HELD TODAY, DECISION
SCHOOLS WILL REMAIN CLOSED, ALSO PLACES OF AMUSEMENT

Soldiers shared a meal at Fort Snelling's mess hall in this photo taken in about 1918. Minneapolis health officials advised against gathering in enclosed spaces such as this, where the contagion could easily move from person to person. *Courtesy of the Minnesota Historical Society.*

The influenza lid went on in Minneapolis at midnight last night.

Not a single service will be held in any Minneapolis church today. The schools will not open tomorrow morning. Theaters, dance halls, pool halls and other meeting places closed at midnight to remain closed until the health department revokes its order, made as an emergency measure to stop the spread of Spanish influenza.

Downtown theaters were packed last night with patrons who took advantage of their last chance to see a performance until the ban is lifted. Long lines of men and women waited in front of the motion picture and vaudeville theaters during the early hours of the evening.

CHURCHES TO CLOSE.

Pastors last night said the health department's order closing the churches would be obeyed to the letter. No mass will be said in the Catholic churches today. Many of the Protestant congregations will spend the hour usually devoted to church services at home in thanksgiving worship for the recent Allied victories.

Four hundred and twelve new cases of influenza were reported to the health department yesterday. The number is incomplete, Dr. Guilford, city health commissioner, said last night, because many physicians do not report their Saturday afternoon cases until Monday. Four deaths occurred yesterday. Idol Olson of New Rockford, N.D.; Alfred Griswold, St. James hotel, and Ernest Whcfscl, 1500 Stevens avenue, died at the City hospital. Private Clinton Rice of Columbia, Mo., a member of the Twenty-ninth battalion, United States guards, stationed at Fort Snelling, died at the fort yesterday afternoon.

Twelve civilians suffering with influenza were admitted to the City hospital yesterday. Twelve nurses at the hospital were taken ill with the epidemic and were quarantined. The university hospital is to be used only for influenza cases, civilians included, according to action taken by the board of regents yesterday. Sixteen new cases were admitted to the military hospital at Fort Snelling where the total now is 390. Seventy men were released. One new case was reported in the Dunwoody naval training detachment yesterday, Lieut. Colby Dodge said last night.

"U" OPENING POSTPONED.

The board of regents of the University yesterday again postponed the opening of the university to civilian students, save to those in the colleges of medicine, dentistry and pharmacy, provided they live under regulations imposed by the health service. A committee, consisting of Pierce Butler, president of the board of regents, President Burton and Dr. J.C. Sundwall, director of the university health service, was appointed and given authority to decide when the university will be opened to civilian students. Their decision will depend upon the abatement of the epidemic. The university high school has been closed until further notice.

While expressing surprise that the schools were included in the health department's influenza closing order, the board of education yesterday formally approved the order and directed that the schools be closed indefinitely.

Health officials pointed out last night that the order has only to do with places of public assemblage and has no bearing on business houses, as it is not felt there is the same likelihood of infection in commercial institutions.

Dr. Richard O. Beard, assistant dean of the university medical school, in approving last night the preventative measures of the health department, emphasized one factor which he felt Dr. Guilford had not emphasized strongly enough—that of fresh air.

Fresh Air Antidote.

"The micro-organisms of disease," Dr. Beard said, "distributed by mouth or nose-spray from the air passages of one person to those of another, are diluted and their dose is, as it were, diminished by an abundance of fresh air. The crowd in the street car, the school, the church or the theater, is a menace because infected individuals concentrate in a limited air space the germs of the disease.

"Let the people learn these large lessons of prevention: Work in a cool, constantly ventilated department. Walk rather than ride. Ride, if you must, in an open air conveyance. Button up wraps and overcoats and open wide the windows of the street car however cold it may be. Sleep as nearly as possible out of doors. Under these precautions, the chances of influenza infection will be materially lessened."

Fifty vaudeville actors, who will arrive in Minneapolis today for a week's run in local theaters, are due for an unsolicited vacation. All actors booked to play at the Orpheum, Grand and Pantages theaters have been ordered to come to Minneapolis regardless of the order and to remain here until the ban is lifted, when they will begin playing at their respective theaters. The Metropolitan, Gayety and Palace theaters will not be affected in this respect, as their acts come here from St. Paul. St. Paul managers will be responsible for booking the acts that were to have appeared here this week.

J.L. Murphy, grand knight of the Hennepin-Minneapolis council, Knights of Columbus, has called off a meeting to have been held at the club house tonight in observance of Columbus Day and the regular council meeting tomorrow night.

Red Cross Meeting Off.

The annual meeting of the Minneapolis chapter of the Red Cross, to have been held on October 23, has been postponed indefinitely because of the epidemic. Dr. T.S. Roberts has replaced Dr. Arthur C. Strachauer as chairman of the influenza committee of the Minneapolis chapter. The committee now consists of Dr. Roberts, Miss Minnie Paterson, Mrs. E.L. Carpenter, Paul Benjamin and C.P. Crangle.

The Minneapolis Athletic club last night canceled its boxing program, its scheduled dancing and all preparations for a Halloween party.

Minneapolis dance halls such as the Arcadia Palace on Fifth Street were ordered closed until further notice. *Courtesy of the Minnesota Historical Society.*

The police were ordered yesterday to prohibit crowds from gathering in the saloons. No loitering will be permitted.

Mail carriers will co-operate with the health organizations in stopping the spread of influenza, the Anti-tuberculosis committee announced yesterday. The carriers will distribute special literature at every house and office at which they leave mail tomorrow. Boy Scouts are being mobilized and will be put into action tomorrow distributing placards and literature to all stores, offices and factories in the downtown district.

Less than 30 new cases were reported in St. Paul yesterday. There were no deaths.

HUNDREDS DIE IN CLOQUET FIRE

OCTOBER 14, 1918, *MINNEAPOLIS MORNING TRIBUNE*

*O*ctober 1918 must have felt apocalyptic to Minnesotans. Lists of servicemen killed in the bloody Great War filled a column a day in the local papers. The deadly Spanish flu was filling hospitals and emptying churches, theaters and dance halls. Then, on October 12 and 13, huge fires exploded in the forests of central Minnesota and swept east toward Lake Superior, incinerating everything in their path. The final toll: 453 people killed, 85 seriously burned, 1,500 square miles blackened, more than ten thousand families displaced and dozens of communities destroyed, including Cloquet, Kettle River and Moose Lake.

Railroads were credited with saving thousands of lives in a massive evacuation. But courts eventually held railroads responsible for the tragedy: Sparks from trains ignited dry grass and piles of wood along the tracks.

Here's the first report on the fire in the Morning Tribune:

FLAMES DEATH TOLL 1,000 IN NORTHERN MINNESOTA; MOOSE LAKE, CLOQUET AND 8 OTHER TOWNS DESTROYED
TERRITORY 21 MILES WIDE SWEPT; PROPERTY LOSS UP IN MILLIONS SURVIVORS RELATE GRAPHIC TALES OF MANY REFUGEES STRICKEN AS THEY SEEK SAFETY

Nearly 1,000 persons are now believed to have lost their lives in the blasts of flame that drove Saturday and yesterday over Northern Minnesota forests in an area that spreads from Duluth to Brainerd, Bemidji, Aitkin, Cloquet and Moose Lake.

The fast-moving fire left the town of Cloquet in ruins. *Courtesy of the Carlton County Historical Society.*

Property worth millions of dollars was destroyed, ten villages were obliterated, 15,000 persons were made homeless, many of them penniless. Duluth, itself heavily damaged by the flames, was last night a city of thousands of refugees, a dwelling-place of stricken people who had lost kinfolk, friends, neighbors in the flames.

Over all the countryside, on highways and by-paths, near farmhouse ruins and beside railway tracks, lay blackened corpses.

100 BODIES BROUGHT IN FROM COUNTRYSIDE.
Cloquet, city of 9,000 population and long a lumber center of the North Country, is all but wiped out. Moose Lake, village of 1,000 souls, is a waste of ashes, a relief-party headquarters which last night held more than 100 bodies brought in from the countryside which held none knew how many other victims stricken as they fled.

Brookston, Brevator, Corona, Adolph, Thompson, Arnold, Wright and Kettle River are in ashes—blackened, smoking wastes hardly distinguishable from the blackened fields that surround them. And all about, the forests of Northern Minnesota stand a great field of burned pine trees—blackened of trunk, ghosts of the great forest.

300 DEAD AT MOOSE LAKE, OFFICIALS ESTIMATE.
Rescue parties arriving on the scene late last night, appalled at the completeness of the devastation wrought by the flames, hesitated, in view of their fragmentary knowledge of the actual scope of the disaster, to estimate the number of dead. In a temporary morgue at Moose Lake there were at midnight 103 bodies. Officials there say the total will exceed 300.

At a late hour last night 196 bodies had been borne to Duluth morgues. In other districts, it was reported that several hundred more may be added. And in addition to these, remains the work of searching among the ruins of burned homes and along the sideroads, where hundreds more may be found, military authorities said.

The fire started near Bemidji, where fire has been smouldering for weeks. Fanned by a high wind, the flames swept across the state toward Duluth, cutting a swath 50 miles wide through cutover lands bounded on both sides by a chain of lakes.

At Moose Lake the havoc wrought by the blaze was most complete, although the loss of life in the town itself was low, because the inhabitants, warned of the approach of the fire, took refuge in the icy waters of the lake.

Brainerd, Bemidji and Aitkin escaped destruction partly because the wind died down and in part through heroic work of volunteer fire fighters.

Duluth and Superior, although suburbs were burned, were untouched by the flames and today are serving as a place of refuge for a large number of the 15,000 homeless ones.

The heaviest loss of life was at Moose Lake and vicinity. Adjutant General Rhinow estimating that more than 300 persons died there. Duluth morgues have approximately 200 bodies and officials estimate that several hundred more dead men, women and children are scattered throughout the fire region.

HIBBING RINGED BY FIRE.
Hibbing, although ringed about fire, was unharmed. Citizens of the Iron range were last night hurrying for shelter at Carlton, and fires were blazing at the Morton location, Keewatin and other towns. Grand Rapids was reported on fire.

Five mills are all that is left today in Cloquet of what was yesterday a city of 9,000 persons with varied business interests and many

Terrified motorists tried to find refuge in the chilly waters of Moose Lake. It's unknown whether the occupants of these cars survived. *Courtesy of the Minnesota Historical Society.*

beautiful homes. The homes are a smouldering ruin, every residence being burned, but warning of the approaching fire came in time to allow the people of the town to depart.

Twelve trains of the Northern Pacific railroad were made up at Carlton when it became known that there was no chance to save the town. The trains were of a nondescript nature, some passenger coaches, some box cars and flat cars, onto which the townspeople were loaded bound for Duluth.

State authorities, headed by Governor Burnquist, who joined the third relief expedition which departed last night for Moose Lake, and commanded on the field by Adjutant General Rhinow, are taking relief to the stricken districts and their people.

The Red Cross responded by dispatching a special train with doctors and nurses and the motor corps of the whole power of the state.

Adjutant General Rhinow and his staff, first of the rescue parties to reach Moose Lake, arrived there yesterday at 5:30 p.m. Their first work was to establish a temporary morgue in a building that partially escaped the flames. At midnight it held 102 bodies. The injured had been sent by special train to Duluth, 30 miles away.

Rescue work was halted at midnight, to be resumed again at daybreak today. The task of probing into the ruins of homes in search of bodies, and of looking beneath the charred remains of automobiles, which are scattered along every roadside, will engage the time of the Home Guards and the members of the motor corps for several days, it is expected.

MOTOR CORPS ON GROUND.

Colonel Stevens, in command of the motor corps, arrived at Moose Lake, which is relief headquarters, shortly after 6 o'clock. The 33 cars under his command arrived within a short time. Members of the motor corps and Adjutant General Rhinow's staff were the only Minneapolis Home Guards on the scene. Other guards were there from Hinckley, North Branch, Iron City and Rock creek. These men will today help to man the ambulance cars, which are part of the motor corps equipment.

First estimates from an official source of the loss of life in the forest fires placed the total deaths in the Moose Lake region alone at more than 200.

Adjutant General Rhinow, who spent last night in the stricken village, telephoned this figure to the capitol early today.

Adjutant General Rhinow, who has charge of law and order and the direction of relief work in the devastated zone, said that

Bodies were lowered into a mass grave outside what was left of the town of Moose Lake. *Courtesy of the Minnesota Historical Society.*

at midnight the fire was fairly under control. He characterized the relief work as well organized and said that all immediate wants were supplied.

MORGUES FILLED WITH BODIES.
Three improvised morgues in Moose Lake buildings which escaped the flames hold the bodies of 80 victims—burned beyond recognition.

Many persons who suffered burns in fleeing from the fires are being cared for by Major F.J. Plondke, St. Paul, and his medical staff and an adequate corps of nurses.

Bodies of 17 men, women and children, literally baked to death in a root cellar on a farm about four miles west of Moose Lake, were among the horrifying finds reported last night.

TARRED AND FEATHERED

NOVEMBER 16, 1919, *MINNEAPOLIS TRIBUNE*

*A*nti-German sentiment was widespread in the United States in the final two years of World War I. German-language newspapers were shuttered, lists of "disloyal" German-Americans were published in newspapers, "pro-German" books were burned and vigilantes attacked German immigrants.

On August 19, 1918, a group of Luverne, Minnesota, men forced their way into a house belonging to the family of John Meints, a German-American farmer they considered to be disloyal to the United States. They removed him forcibly and drove him by car to the South Dakota border, where masked men "assaulted him, whipped him, threatened to shoot him, besmeared his body with tar and feathers, and told him to cross the line into South Dakota, and that if he ever returned to Minnesota he would be hanged," court records show.

Meints sued thirty-two of the men involved, seeking damages of $100,000 for false imprisonment. After a lengthy trial in Mankato that produced more than 1,100 pages of testimony, a U.S. District Court jury ruled for the defendants, prompting the giddy homecoming described below in a page-one story in the Tribune. Meints—not "Meintz," as this disappointingly short piece has it—won a new trial on appeal and eventually settled out of court in 1922 for $6,000.

ALL LUVERNE GREETS 32 CITIZENS FREED IN TAR-FEATHER CASE
COURT VINDICATES MEN ACCUSED OF PUNISHING JOHN MEINTZ AS DISLOYALIST

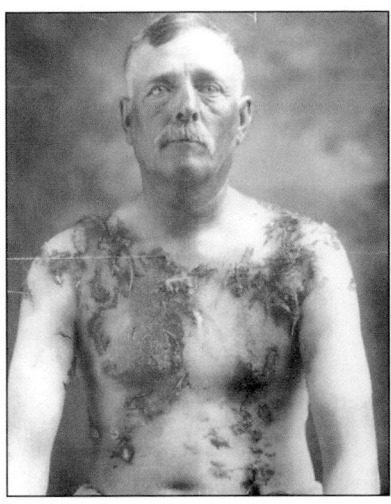

Exhibit A: John Meints.

Welcome home by a large delegation of Luverne (Minn.) citizens, headed by a band, was the sequel yesterday to the acquittal of 32 residents in federal court at Mankato on the charge of kidnapping, tarring and feathering John Meintz, according to dispatches from Luverne last night.

Meintz asked personal damages of $100,000 as balm for the treatment he received on the night of August 19, 1918. The jury denied him any damages, after deliberating one hour and a half.

Judge Wilbur F. Booth, in charging the jury, said that the evidence was overwhelming in support of the contention that Meintz was disloyal and that there was a strong feeling against him in the community.

The action of the Luverne citizens in staging a celebration was taken as an indication of strong approval of the acquittal verdict, according to dispatches.

AN ORGAN GRINDER'S DESPAIR

JANUARY 22, 1922, *MINNEAPOLIS TRIBUNE*

*B*ylines were rare in Twin Cities newspapers of the 1920s. Women's bylines were rarer still. And any woman who specialized in first-person feature stories—as the Tribune's Lorena A. Hickok did—was likely to be referred to as a "girl reporter" in the accompanying headlines.

Hickok, a native of East Troy, Wisconsin, wrote scores of stories for the Tribune in the early 1920s. She endured a lot of hokey first-person assignments—or maybe she gravitated toward them. She allowed herself to be hypnotized by a vaudevillian performer. She filled in for a department store Santa. She covered a "secret" Gophers football practice, using her professed ignorance of the game to get a foot in the door at a "rehearsal" before a big game with the University of Wisconsin Badgers. But she also scored entertaining and insightful interviews with polar explorer Roald Amundsen and pianist Sergei Rachmaninoff. Her writing shows wit, sensitivity and a flair for the dramatic—although the story below might seem a bit purple to the modern reader.

Hickok went on to write for the Associated Press, covering the Lindbergh kidnapping and Franklin D. Roosevelt's run for president in 1932. During that assignment, "Hick" hit it off with Eleanor Roosevelt, and the two developed a close friendship that lasted until Roosevelt's death in 1962. The intimate letters they exchanged over the years have prompted much speculation about the depth of their relationship, but historians remain divided on whether the two were romantically involved.

Hurdy Gurdy Man, Already Deep in Despair, Told Wife Is Dying
Grief Over Demise of Pet Monkey Accentuated By Greater Tragedy.

By Lorena A. Hickok

Jenny, Carmen Biondi's performing monkey, is dead.

Wherefore the heart of Carmen Biondi, the old hurdy gurdy man, is heavy with grief and impotent despair.

And from her bed in the General hospital yesterday, Rafella Biondi, Carmen's wife, swore eternal vengeance upon the villains who abducted Jenny from her master's home, tied her up in a cold wood shed, and let her die there—of cold and hunger.

Carmen was not doing any cursing yesterday, however. He had no heart for revenge. For another tragedy reared its grisly head above Carmen's black horizon and threatened to crush him with a sorrow that would make him forget even the loss of his pet.

Told Wife Is Dying.

When Carmen went to the hospital yesterday morning to see his wife, he was told that she was dying—that she would never return alive to the little tar-paper shack out at 648 Johnson street northeast, where drying herbs and red peppers hang in bundles from the ceiling, and where she used to sing the long winter evenings through while Carmen ground the music of sunny Italy out of his old hand-organ.

From her death-bed, Rafella Biondi directed that a reward of $10 be offered to anybody who caught the suspected abductors of Jenny trespassing on Carmen's property again.

She instructed Carmen to pay this reward out of "monkey money" deposited in the St. Anthony Falls bank—money earned by Carmen and his pets in happier days gone by and turned over to her.

Pet Disappears From Home.

Jenny disappeared from her cage the afternoon of January 10, while her master was down at the hospital visiting his wife. Yesterday he said her body had been found, stiff and cold, in a woodshed. Her kidnapers, Carmen said, had tied her there and let her die of hunger and exposure.

An organ grinder and his monkey worked the streets of Minneapolis in about 1910. *Courtesy of the Hennepin County Library, Minneapolis Collection.*

For more than 20 years Carmen has gone with his organ on summer Sunday afternoons to the Minneapolis parks and to the summer homes at Lake Minnetonka to play for the children. Often in those happy days he was accompanied by Rafella, who used to laugh delightedly at the antics of the "lit-tla ones."

That was his play, however—he called it his "idle work." He earned his living mainly by working in the city sewer department. Last summer he found that the work was getting pretty heavy for him—he will be 60 years old on his next birthday.

So he sent to Brazil for Jenny, a ring-tail monkey, and Mike, her mate. For six months he had been training them to dance and bow and pass the little tin cup, while he ground the "Marseillaiseee" and haunting melodies from "Il Trovatore" and "La Traviata" out of his old hand-organ.

MIKE NOT HIMSELF SINCE.

And then Jenny disappeared. Mike has never been himself, Carmen says, since they took Jenny away. He refuses to eat, and shows no inclination whatever to try his stunts—nor has Carmen the heart to make him try. They spend much of their time huddled together on the edge of the tumbled bed in Carmen's shack—discussing, in musical Italian and shrill monkey jargon, the fate of Jenny and the fate they wish would befall Jenny's abductors.

Carmen came from the hospital to tell me about it yesterday.

"I finda my monk," he said, when I went out to talk to him. "Dead. She die in da shed. Hungry. Cold. Breaks my heart.

"And my Rafella—she die, too. Never getta well. Never come home again. I play no more. I sella my organ."

Carmen pulled out a little blue paper—a perpetual pass into the ward where his wife is. He pointed to it and said:

"Put in a paper, please—nobody can see my Rafella. Too sick, now. Nobody see her—only me."

He stood silent for a long time, gazing at the floor. His eyelids, I noticed them, were red and swollen. I said nothing—there wasn't anything to say. At length he looked up, held out his hand, and said brokenly:

"Good-bye, lady. I go home. Tella Mike. Gooda-bye."

BOHEMIAN FLATS WOMEN DEFY EVICTION

MAY 25, 1923, *MINNEAPOLIS MORNING TRIBUNE*

*F*or more than half a century, the river flats below the Washington Avenue bridge on the Mississippi's west bank were an entry point for immigrants new to Minneapolis. Housing was cheap, but it was a hard life. Utilities were spartan at best, and spring floods regularly forced people out of the cheapest shanties next to the river.

Bohemian Flats, as it came to be known, began to lose residents in the 1920s, when landowners demanded they pay rent or move out. By the early 1930s, only a few houses remained; the others had been torn down to make way for a barge terminal. The last resident held on, somehow, for another thirty years, living in the shadow of oil tanks and piles of coal. The barge terminal has since been replaced by Bohemian Flats Park.

Following is a Morning Tribune *account of a tense confrontation between the women of the flats—the men were at work—and police bearing a court order for their eviction.*

WIVES HOLD RIVER FLAT HOMES WHEN POLICE ATTEMPT EVICTION
SQUATTERS WIN TEMPORARILY WITH WRIT ORDERING STAY OF EJECTION MOVE.
RESIDENTS REFUSE TO PAY FOR GROUND LEASE—ORDERED IN COURT TUESDAY.

Residents of the Mississippi river flats fought for the squatter sovereignty of their homes under the Washington avenue bridge Thursday, and emerged temporarily victorious.

Women of the flats stood guard over their thresholds while police attempted to eject them for failure to pay rent on the grounds on which the dwellings stand. A near-riot was halted when a second court order was served on police, ordering a stay of the ejections.

SECOND ORDER REVIVES HOPES.

Furniture from the home of Joseph Filek and from that of John Medvec, pioneer of the river colony, was being piled into moving vans when Mrs. Medvec, 57 years old, fainted. Dr. J.L. Everlof, 1501 Washington avenue south, was called and the woman was revived, but she was hysterical until the second court order brought hope that her home might be restored.

Under the latest order the contending parties must appear in municipal court at 10 a.m. Tuesday for a determination of the case. Title to the property is held by C.H. Smith, Phoenix building. Acting in his behalf, Clinton A. Rehnke, attorney, appeared on the flats

Bohemian Flats, below the Washington Avenue Bridge, in about 1910. *Courtesy of the Minnesota Historical Society.*

Thursday morning with Police Lieutenant H.M. Burke, and served the ejectment papers on the squatters. They protested.

ANGRY WOMEN DEFY POLICE.

Mrs. Medvec barred the door to her home and defied the police lieutenant to open it. The two men tried to force their way in, and an angry group of women gathered to give aid to Mrs. Medvec. Finally the door was opened and workmen began to pile the furniture into the van. Before they had completed their task David Lundeen, attorney representing the flat dwellers, appeared and served the second order. The furniture went back into the house.

Spokesmen for the flat dwellers announced that, whether or not they are defeated in court, they will refuse to pay the rent. Rather than this, they announced, the colonists will tear down their shacks and move away.

COLONY 60 YEARS OLD.

For nearly 60 years the squatters have settled on the river shore, have built their homes, and each year, during the spring thaws, have fought against the rising waters of the Mississippi.

In 1919 the government high dam project entered as a factor. At that time the land, the rental for which is now in controversy, was owned by a Mary Leland. In an adjustment for the flowage rights which were found necessary because of the construction of the dam, the federal government paid $5,000 to Mary Leland. The squatters looked upon the transaction as a purchase of the land by the government. Mary Leland later transferred her title to Mr. Smith.

SQUATTERS REFUSE TO PAY RENT.

Thereafter some of the dwellers refused to pay rent for the ground and on August 8, 1922, Mr. Smith instituted action in municipal court, seeking to collect the rent or to force the residents to move. The case was continued until September 29, 1922, when Mr. Smith won by default. The flat dwellers failed to appear to explain the merits they believe there was in their cause.

Then followed two court orders of ejectment, both of which died under the law because they were not executed within 20 days. The third writ was issued Thursday.

The women of Bohemian Flats were a resourceful lot. Here, three residents worked to recover a passing log. *Courtesy of the Hennepin County Library, Minneapolis Collection.*

John Medvec, 70 years old, and one of the spokesmen for the flat dwellers, declared he would fight the case to the end.

NO LEASE SIGNED, SAYS SPOKESMAN.

"I've lived here for 38 years," he said. "I bought the place from Mike Balog for $208. I never signed a lease on the ground, and I don't owe anyone any money for rent on the place. It's all mine, and not any one else's."

Similar stories of a determination to fight the case were expressed by John Gabrick, 108 Mill street; Mike Sabol, 109 Mill street; Mrs. John Harhay, 113 Mill street; Mrs. Mike Lash, 105 Wood street, and Mike Rollins, 79 Wood street.

Mr. Smith contends that the flat-dwellers signed leases agreeing to pay rental on the ground. The residents deny the claim. And upon the determination of this issue rests the fate of the river flats.

FRANK LLOYD WRIGHT JAILED IN MINNEAPOLIS

OCTOBER 21, 1926, *MINNEAPOLIS TRIBUNE*

*F*rank Lloyd Wright, one of the most influential American architects of the twentieth century, had his share of personal troubles, many of his own making. His chaotic love life landed him in a Minneapolis jail in October 1926. He was released to the U.S. Marshal's Office the next day, and charges of infidelity and alienation of affection were later dropped. Here is the Tribune's front-page account of the arrest:

FRANK LLOYD WRIGHT JAILED HERE;
FOUND WITH DANCER AT 'TONKA
NOTED ARCHITECT HELD WITHOUT CHARGE FOR BARABOO,
WIS., POLICE.
OCCUPIED COTTAGE AT WILDHURST WITH
MME. OLGA MILANOFF SINCE SEPT. 7.

Frank Lloyd Wright, an architect of international fame, who has been dodging the courts on various counts since September 1, when he eluded Chicago and Milwaukee authorities, was arrested by Hennepin county deputy sheriffs Wednesday night in a cottage at Wildhurst, Lake Minnetonka. He was brought to the Hennepin county jail, where he was held without charge for Baraboo, Wis., authorities.

With Mr. Wright, the husband of Miriam Noel Wright, from whom he is estranged, was Mme. Olga Milanoff, a Montenegrin dancer, whose husband has been searching for her with the same

Wright was arrested at the kitchen door of a Lake Minnetonka cottage on October 20, 1926. The woman directly behind him probably was the cook, Viola Meyerhaus. *Courtesy of the Hennepin County Library, Minneapolis Collection.*

diligence with which Mrs. Wright sought the architect. They were occupying the cottage with two children, Svetlana, 9 years old, the dancer's daughter by her husband, Vladimir Hinzenburg, an 18-month-old baby, [the infant, a girl, was actually ten months old] a stenographer and a maid. After arresting Wright the deputies returned to Minnetonka and brought Mme. Milanoff and the two children to the county jail.

RENTED COTTAGE SEPTEMBER 7.
It developed that Mr. Wright came to Lake Minnetonka September 7, and rented the cottage on the shores of 'Tonka bay belonging to Mrs. D.F. Simpson, widow of the late Judge Simpson. He paid the rental in advance and in currency. It was said that he retained the domestic help employed by the Simpsons, and went further to ask Mrs. Simpson if he might use her name in procuring meats and groceries. This was refused.

Wright's lover, dancer Olga Milanoff, and their daughter, Iovanna. *Courtesy of the Hennepin County Library, Minneapolis Collection.*

Apparently he and Mme. Milanoff have lived at the cottage for more than six weeks. Mr. Wright has been engaged in completing the first of two volumes of an autobiography.

When the deputies came to the kitchen door of the cottage Wednesday night they were met by the cook and maid, Miss Viola Meyerhaus. They asked for "Mr. Richardson," having obtained knowledge that Mr. Wright used that alias in Chicago, and were admitted. Wright at first denied his identity, but later admitted that he was the man they sought.

NERVOUS AT FIRST.

At first he exhibited nervousness and anxiety, but after his admission he settled back calmly and answered their questions.

Mme. Milanoff is the wife of a Chicago architect. She became Wright's housekeeper, and, according to Mrs. Wright, is "the one who broke up our home." Mr. Wright owns a large estate, Taliesen, near Spring Green, Wis.

"Is this my country and is this what I have worked for?" asked the architect at the Hennepin county jail Wednesday night. "Can't I be left alone? Everyone I see, except those I love, reminds me of the hog that trampled down the corn it couldn't eat.

"I have lived an honorable life. Is it at all fair to the baby to deny her what my love for her deserves. My fortunes and my destinies do not count at all. It is just that child."

Shortly after Mr. Wright declared to a questioner that he had never denied being the father of the baby, whom he and Mme. Milanoff call "Pussy." He would make no admissions further than that.

At the Simpson cottage Svetlana broke into tears. Mme. Olga, who had been sitting quietly in the living room, while a stenographer typed the latest passages dictated to her by her employer, took the child into her arms and advanced toward the men.

Frank Lloyd Wright and his daughter, Iovanna. *Courtesy of the Hennepin County Library, Minneapolis Collection.*

Child Is Frightened.

"Tell my child that nothing is wrong. She is frightened and her heart will break. Tell her that all will be right tomorrow." And each of the men did.

The child, when asked her name, had replied that it was "Mary." The cook, Viola Meyerhaus, declared that she had been called "Mary" by her mother and by Wright, but added that all her dresses were monogrammed "Svetlana."

Wright said that he had come to Lake Minnetonka in search of complete rest and to complete his autobiography. He said he had no knowledge of the fact that he was charged with infidelity by his wife and alienation of affections by Olga's husband. The same charges had been preferred against Mme. Milanoff by Mrs. Wright and Hinzenberg.

May Fight Extradition.

Only once did Wright refer to his work in architecture, which has brought him international prominence. Then he said:

1928		22	Robert	Woodroof	"	39	5	7
1929	U.S.M	23	Peter	Obedahl	"	25	5	4
1930		24	Dan	Robertson	"	15	5	5
1931	U.S.M	25	Frank L.	Wright	"	58	5	9
1932	U.S.M	26	Olga	Hinzenberg	female	36	5	2
1933		27	Merrill A.	Schute	male	40	5	10
1934		28	Ingolf	Ellstrom	"	26	5	9

A detail of the jail log in Minneapolis that night shows the names of Wright (age fifty-eight, five feet, nine inches) and Hinzenberg (Olga's married name). *Courtesy of the Minnesota Historical Society.*

"I had a letter from a girl reporter in Tokio. She said that the Imperial hotel there was the only thing in the Orient which had lived up to her expectations. I designed and constructed that hotel, even all the furniture."

It is probable that Wright will fight extradition. Attorneys for his defense will arrive from Milwaukee today, he said, after communicating with them Wednesday night. Chicago attorneys for both Mrs. Wright and Hinzenberg are also expected.

The romance of Wright and Maude Miriam Noel Wright, sculptress, which started with their flight to Japan 12 years ago, ended last December when she filed suit for divorce in Baraboo, Wis., charging desertion and cruelty. They were married in 1922, it then became known, a day after Mr. Wright had obtained a divorce from Mrs. Catherine L. Wright of Oak Park, Ill.

With Mme. Milanoff, Wright eluded the authorities at Baraboo.

The charges were brought by Hinzenberg, divorced husband of Mme. Milanoff, who was attempting to secure custody of his 9-year-old daughter. The child had been awarded to Mme. Milanoff at the time of the divorce.

Since September 1 no trace of Wright and Mme. Milanoff had been found. On September 30 it was reported that Wright was in Mexico, this report being based on a letter from him there said to have been received by a Chicago attorney, who was his personal friend.

ST. PAUL GANG FIGURE SLAIN

DECEMBER 5, 1928, *MINNEAPOLIS MORNING TRIBUNE*

*T*hanks to Prohibition, criminal gangs plagued the Twin Cities in the 1920s and '30s. A corrupt St. Paul Police Department provided safe haven to gangsters and crooks of the era, as long as they agreed to stay out of trouble while in the city. The task of keeping the bad boys in line fell to "Dapper Dan" Hogan, a speakeasy owner and underworld leader. On December 4, 1928, Hogan, "whose word was known to be law among many criminals," was killed by a car bomb in the garage behind his St. Paul home. Rival gangsters were the likely culprits, but his murder was never officially solved.

DANNY HOGAN SLAIN; VICTIM OF AUTO BOMB
BLAST NEARLY TEARS OFF LEG OF TWIN CITIES UNDERWORLD LORD.
RACKETEERS VAINLY OFFER BLOOD FOR TRANSFUSION TO SAVE CHIEF.
POLICE KEEP LOOKOUT FOR POSSIBLE REPRISALS BY LEADER'S FRIENDS.

The victim of a bomb which exploded his automobile, Danny Hogan, St. Paul restaurant proprietor and a well known figure in the Twin Cities underworld, died shortly before 9 p.m. Tuesday in the St. Paul hospital, while police were seeking the men who murdered him and were watching for attempts at reprisals.

Hogan, a figure in many police investigations, and whose word was known to have been law among many criminals, was fatally injured Tuesday morning as he was attempting to drive his automobile out of the garage in back of his home at 1607 West Seventh street, St. Paul. The bomb, which very nearly tore off his right leg, presumably was detonated when Hogan pressed his foot to the starter.

Unable to Name Assailants.

Fragments of the bomb, missing his right foot entirely, entered the leg at the ankle and continued upward to the knee. The bone of the leg was pulverized. Other fragments severely lacerated his right arm, and tore off the ring finger. He suffered one deep cut over the right eye. The underworld leader died without being able to name his assailants.

"I don't know what happened or why it happened," he said in a brief statement to Edward Diehl, assistant Ramsey county attorney. "I touched the starter and that's all I remember. I don't know who could have done it. I didn't know I had an enemy in the world."

Rumors had been current among underworld members of St. Paul for several days that "someone was marked for death." One theory held by police is that Hogan was killed by gambling racketeers. He is said to have been connected with a gambling house near Mendota which was closed recently.

Found Unconscious.

In soft drink bars, cigar stores and small hotels of St. Paul, where underworld characters congregate, there were rumors Tuesday night that vengeance would result from the Hogan killing. Police understood that they would have aid from a lawless element in tracking down of the killers.

The blast occurred at about 11:30 a.m. Tuesday. Hogan had gone into the garage to take out his car. His aged father-in-law, F.D. Hardy, 73 years old, was to have accompanied him. The two men had just finished a late breakfast and were going to drive to downtown St. Paul. When Hardy reached the garage he remembered a money order which he had left in the house, so he returned to get it.

A short time afterwards there was a loud explosion. When neighbors and members of the family entered the garage they found Hogan unconscious in the seat of the car, his right leg nearly torn off, and bleeding profusely.

Blast Wrecks Auto.

The explosive, believed to have been placed directly underneath the floor boards of the machine, and wired to the starter, had blown the boards to bits, shattered windows in the car and torn open its cowling. A large hole was made in the top of the automobile and the steering wheel was blown completely off its post. Holes in the steel sides of the car body showed where bits of metal had been buried through with the velocity of bullets. Detectives searching the scene of the crime later found bits of soft metal scattered about the wrecked car. The hood of the machine was blown off, but the engine was not wrecked.

A police ambulance was dispatched to the scene immediately and Dr. F.L. Webber, police surgeon, found Hogan still unconscious. At the hospital, Hogan's right leg was amputated in an effort to save his life. It soon became apparent that blood transfusions also would be necessary.

RACKETEERS OFFERED BLOOD.

From all walks of life, the friends of the underworld chief, who was known as "Dapper Dan," came to the hospital to offer their services for blood transfusions. Among them were racketeers, police characters and business men. These proffers of assistance were an indication of the esteem in which the murdered man was held by many people of the Twin Cities.

Hogan's condition became progressively more serious during the day and death came shortly before 9 p.m.

Police Chief E.J. Murnane and Captain of Detectives Herman Vall, St. Paul, took personal charge of the investigation of the crime. They have ordered every detective on the force to hunt for Hogan's assailants.

WIFE SAW MYSTERY PAIR.

Mrs. Hogan reported that at 6 a.m. Tuesday she saw two men drive up and stop near the Hogan garage. She did not know the men and paid no attention to them. Police believe that it was these two men who entered the garage and planted the bomb. The assassins, according to police, evidently know well Hogan's habits, as there was a second car in the garage, a large sedan. The car in which Hogan was fatally injured was a coupe and the men evidently knew that this was the machine he was in the habit of using.

Detectives searched the sedan to determine whether a bomb had been planted in it, also, but they found nothing. The explosive used in the coupe was nitroglycerine, which is both highly powerful and easily concealed.

Hogan was arrested by police in January, 1927, for alleged participation in a $35,000 mail robbery in South St. Paul. Arrested with him were Frank W. Sommer, former St. Paul police chief and secret service official; George E. Blaul, former agent at South St. Paul, and Reuben C. Lilley, alias "Black" Carter.

FRIENDS PUT UP $100,000.

Hogan's bond was fixed at $100,000, a record sum, but here again his friends rallied to his support and within a short time 25 bondsmen had put up the sum.

The cases against Hogan and Sommer were dismissed July 5, 1927, by Federal Judge Andrew Miller. The dismissal was on defense motion, presented a month earlier when the government announced it was unable to proceed with the prosecution. The case against the men was understood to have fallen down when a star witness for the prosecution made a sworn statement that charges against the defendants had been hatched at Leavenworth penitentiary by Terry Moran, one of the bandits convicted of complicity in the mail robbery. Moran later was killed while an inmate of the federal prison at Atlanta.

POWER IN UNDERWORLD.

"Dapper Dan" was known throughout the northwest, and in many other places throughout the United States, as a man who had the power to settle feudal wars and "keep the heat out of town." He is known to have told criminals, on many occasions, that they could stay in St. Paul as long as they behaved and started no "racket." Police knew that he had frequently ordered thieves and gangsters out of the Twin Cities and sometimes gave them money so that they "might be on their way."

He was the idol of not a few persons and his word was said to have been "as good as a gold bond." To numbers of persons he was something of a Robin Hood. There will be some fewer turkey dinners in St. Paul this Christmas as a result of his death, according to the talk in the soft drink bars in St. Paul Tuesday night.

O'DOWD OFFERS AID.

Among the several score persons who waited in the ante-room of the hospital Tuesday afternoon for the chance to give blood to the dying man was Mike O'Dowd, former professional boxer, and at one time middleweight champion of the world.

Hogan was conscious and smiling throughout the operation of amputation. When Dr. Arnold F. Plankers, the surgeon summoned to do the operating, appeared in the room, Hogan said "hello" and told him blandly that he "better do his best." He scorned a general anaesthetic and submitted to the amputation with only a local anaesthetic.

In the evening, when Hogan appeared stronger, preparations were made for a blood transfusion, but he sank into a coma and died at 8:55 p.m.

Inside of 15 minutes, the word of his death was passed around the city by "grapevine telephone," and the hospital, police headquarters and newspapers were besieged with hundreds of calls from the dead man's friends. Police, at that time, were bending every effort to discover Hogan's murderers and prevent vengeance by the underworld chief's friends.

GANGSTER MUST GO.
Rumors are current in St. Paul that the crime was committed by New York gunmen, experts in the newest form of bomb killing, hired by a gang of Minneapolis gamblers.

Police up to a late hour Tuesday night had only two clues on which to work, one the description of the two men seen in the rear of the Hogan home early Tuesday, and the other the fragments of the bomb taken from the garage, Hogan's leg and his arm.

"The gangster must go," Chief Murnane asserted Tuesday night after a day of major crime in St. Paul in which a murder was committed, a former policeman shot as a burglar, and a filling station robbed by a bandit who fired at the attendant.

"If there are gangsters or undesirables in the city they certainly will be cleaned out," the chief said. "The gangster must go. We intend to enforce the laws and give St. Paul the best possible policing under existing conditions."

RACE ROW IN MINNEAPOLIS

JULY 16, 1931, *MINNEAPOLIS TRIBUNE*

*I*n June 1931, Arthur and Edith Lee bought a two-bedroom bungalow at 4600 Columbus Avenue in south Minneapolis. The Lees were black, the neighborhood white. Despite threats from the neighborhood association, they moved into the home in July, along with their six-year-old daughter. A group of neighbors offered to buy the home back for $300 more than the Lees had paid. The family declined.

"Nobody asked me to move out when I was in France fighting in mud and water for this country," Arthur Lee, a World War I veteran, told the Tribune. "I came out here to make this house my home. I have a right to establish a home."

In mid-July, thousands of white people assembled nightly at Forty-sixth and Columbus in protest, many hurling taunts and rocks at the home. Friends gathered in the Lee home to show their support. Police stood outside, urging the crowds to disperse as tensions rose. On Friday, July 17, an end to the "race row" appeared near. The Tribune reported "definite progress" in negotiations over the sale of the house and said it appeared that Lee would move soon, perhaps within a week. The protests waned, but neighbors continued to pressure the Lees to move. Years later, they finally sold the house and moved to another part of the city, but only after waiting long enough to prove they could not be forced out.

The "Miss L.O. Smith" mentioned near the end of the Tribune's dramatic account below is Lena Olive Smith, then president of the Minneapolis branch of the NAACP. Smith, the first black woman licensed to practice law in Minnesota, advised the Lees through much of the conflict. Before earning her law degree, she had practiced dermatology, studied embalming, owned a hair salon and sold real estate.

The story dominated the front pages of Minneapolis newspapers in July 1931.

CROWD OF 3,000 RENEWS ATTACK ON NEGROES' HOME
STONES AGAIN HURLED AT HOUSE ON COLUMBUS AVENUE.
NEIGHBORS WALK OUT OF MEETING WHEN PEACE IS URGED.

While city leaders tried desperately to effect a peaceful settlement of the affair, the rising tide of protest against occupancy of a home at 4600 Columbus avenue by a Negro family Wednesday night resulted in another, more violent demonstration outside the home.

More than 3,000 persons assembled outside the home, occupied by A.A. Lee and his family, to hurl defiance at the police and openly threaten Lee and his friends.

Every available police gun squad was rushed to the scene to keep the crowd under control.

STONES ARE THROWN.
From the windows of his darkened home, Lee and his friends looked out, as from a barricaded fortress, on a sullen, angry semi-circle of humanity. They heard themselves threatened continually, from all directions. They heard stones strike against the house and heard windows crash as some of the stones took effect. Now and then a firecracker exploded on the lawn.

A mass meeting of white home owners of that vicinity, held early in the evening at the Eugene Field school, was apparently unsuccessful. Half of the more than 100 persons who assembled at the school walked out indignantly as speakers were urging patience in the matter.

Edith and Arthur Lee. *Courtesy of the Lee family.*

POLICE GUARD HOME.
"Let's go over to Forty-sixth and Columbus and settle the matter right now," shouted some as they left the meeting.

By the time the meeting was over the Lee home was once

more surrounded by angry home owners, spectators from all parts of the city and a squad of 25 policemen.

During the early part of the evening the police were successful in keeping the crowd moving. Groups were broken up quickly and effectively. By 10:30 p.m., however, the crowd had grown so large that the police were forced to retreat toward the Lee home where they formed a protecting cordon. Standing 10 feet apart, they waited.

PATROLMAN ATTACKED.

Inch by inch the crowd moved closer to the Lee home, muttering threats, and loud in their denunciation of the police. More police reserves were sent for. A squad of motorcycle men mounted their machines. They drove straight at the crowd, turning sharply as they reached the front lines.

This only served to rouse the throng. One motorcycle policeman was pulled from his machine and a squad of patrolmen went charging to his rescue. Word was handed around that someone had struck a woman spectator. There was an ominous roar of disapproval.

Mrs. A.B. Blomberg, 4925 Columbus avenue, was injured in the leg when struck by the machine of a motorcycle patrolman near the scene of the demonstration at the Lee home. She was taken to her home after lacerations were treated by a doctor.

At 11 p.m. a hurry call was sent to police headquarters and every available gun squad car was sent to the scene.

The crowd also was incensed by a practical joke that brought a fire department hose cart and a hook and ladder truck clanging up to the Lee home. The firemen were greeted with a loud chorus of boos by the crowd which took it for granted that the fire department had been called as an emergency measure.

The firemen, plainly confused by their reception, immediately turned their trucks around and left.

By that time the crowd extended along Forty-sixth street from Park to Chicago avenues and for a block along Columbus avenue. Refusing to obey the policemen's orders to stay out of the street they advanced almost to the sidewalks in front of the Lee home, standing almost face to face with the line of policemen. The shrill piping voices of small children were heard over the lower, more deliberate tones of adults.

FIRE HOSE ASKED.

Traffic was blocked completely on Columbus avenue and on Forty-sixth street. Cars were parked for several miles along adjoining streets.

From time to time during the evening groups of Negroes appeared and entered the Lee home. It was estimated that more than 20 friends of the Lee family were assembled in the house at the time the demonstration was at its height.

Toward midnight Captain William Walsh at police headquarters received a call from a man who said he was at the Lee home.

"Send out the fire department and turn a hose on the crowd," the man suggested.

Captain Walsh replied that he had no authority to do that.

By 11:30 p.m. the crowd was in a dangerous mood, ready for any excuse to jeer at the police. When a detective, seeing a youth about to hurl a stone, arrested him, there was a movement toward the detective which was frustrated by the prompt arrival of motorcycle policemen. The youth was hustled into a gun squad car and taken to a precinct station.

The appearance of several Negroes in the crowd also caused a commotion. Police immediately rushed the Negroes to police cars and hurried them away, fearing a racial riot independent of the difficulty regarding the Lee home.

URBAN PRESIDENT SPEAKS.

At the meeting of the Eugene Field school, H.W. Rubins, president of the Urban league, representing Mayor Anderson, pleaded with the assembled home owners to be patient in the affair and to respect as much as possible the principle of property rights.

"This is a time for sanity and patience, not hasty action," he told the assembly. "This government has been founded on certain principles of human and property rights. We must respect those rights."

Rubins had addressed the home owners for a scant 10 minutes when a decided unrest began to evidence itself. Several rose and left the room. Then there was a massed departure which interrupted Rubins. Muttering angrily, those who left their seats hurried from the school to join the crowd outside the Lee home.

Let Committees Work.

To those who remained Rubins continued his address. He pointed out that he was present as an impartial, unbiased observer, in the interest of a satisfactory settlement of the problem. He asked that the committees which have been appointed be given a fair chance to work out a solution to the problem.

Albin J. Lindgren, 4621 Park avenue, chairman of a committee of home owners which has been meeting with a committee appointed by Mayor Anderson and Lee's attorney, presided over the meeting and also urged that residents of the district be patient.

"Let's give the committees a chance," Lindgren suggested, "to see if we can't reach a satisfactory settlement. I suggest that everyone stay away from the corner of Forty-sixth and Columbus tonight."

In July 2011, a marker was placed outside the house to commemorate the eightieth anniversary of the Lees' stand at 4600 Columbus Avenue South.

LEE WON'T MOVE.

Lee himself, in a statement issued through his attorney, H.E. Maag, made it known Wednesday that he has no intention of moving as long as his neighbors continue their demonstrations. He said he is willing to meet with a committee of residents and his attorney and settle the matter in a peaceful manner. Then, he said, after the attention of the city had been diverted from the house he would move quietly to some other part of the city.

Efforts to settle the controversy over Lee's purchase of the home were made Wednesday by interested groups on Mayor Anderson's office. A definite decision was not arrived at.

The Minneapolis Urban league, an organization devoted to the advancement of amicable relations between whites and Negroes, also held a meeting in an effort to mediate the trouble and influence the parties concerned into a settlement.

The National Association For the Advancement of Colored People Wednesday charged the police department with laxity in dispersing what it termed an "unlawful gathering" at the Lee home.

Miss L.O. Smith, president of the Minneapolis branch of the organization, called on Chief of Police William Meehan and charged that the police department had been willfully negligent in its duty in permitting the crowd to form. She said that if the demonstrations continue she will appeal to Governor Olson for aid.

Mayor Anderson, after conferring with representatives of the Negroes and white property owners in the district, asked the latter to "be patient." He asked that some sort of truce be effected pending settlement of the affair.

THE EVIL THAT BOYS DO

MARCH 1, 1939, *MINNEAPOLIS STAR*

When you were a teen, stuck at home with the flu or strep throat, how did you pass the time? I read a lot of books, watched a lot of TV and drank an awful lot of flat 7UP. The fifteen-year-old lad in this story staved off boredom by dialing an awful lot of telephone numbers. The shenanigans earned him a trip to the psychiatrist.

"LOVE THY NEIGHBOR…"
BOYS WILL DO SOME FUNNY THINGS

Boredom and the pangs of thwarted puppy love today had put two Minneapolis residents on record as the most annoyed individuals on earth, a la telephone.

One of these is Mrs. H.N. Buesen, 3856 Thirty-seventh avenue S.

At 11 a.m. yesterday, her doorbell and telephone started to ring. The telephone callers wanted to verify orders for various commodities phoned in for her to commercial houses.

The door callers came with deliveries of diverse articles ALL UNORDERED BY HER.

During the day, she told police, she clocked 75 liquor deliveries, six chow mein deliveries, 35 deliveries of coal or fuel oil, 10 grocery orders, three radio trucks, two refrigerator trucks and a tow car.

By the end of the day she was verging on nervous prostration, but no amount of mental effort could conjure up the name of anyone who would want to pull a trick like that on an unsuspecting neighbor.

Finally she had a thought. The 15-year-old son of a neighboring family had been home from school that day with illness. Police called on him.

HE DENIED EVERYTHING.

In the home telephone directory, however, they found a page had been creased—in the classified section listing liquor stores.

HE ADMITTED MAKING THE CALLS.

He had the friendliest of feelings toward his victim, he said, and didn't want to cause any trouble.

But he simply had telephonitis and was bored stiff after being in the house three or four days.

Sick or not, bored boys are prone to get into trouble. These boys found a happy way to pass the time at General Hospital in Minneapolis in 1946. *Courtesy of the Hennepin County Library, Minneapolis Collection.*

He appeared before Lieut. Magni Palm, juvenile officer, today and was turned over to the child guidance clinic for an examination by a psychiatrist.

The other victim was the father of a girl who had been wooed by a pair of ardent young swains. He told her to tell them not to hang around any more. They didn't, but they wanted to get even.

THEY ORDERED A TON OF COAL SENT TO HIS HOUSE. THE FATHER SENT IT BACK. A PLUMBER ANSWERED A RUSH CALL TO THE HOME AND WAS SENT BACK. NEXT TO APPEAR WAS A PIANO TUNER.

By this time the father was wise.

The two young men were picked up and reprimanded. Their joke, they were told, didn't affect the father so much as it did the merchants and artisans, innocent victims.

ARMISTICE DAY BLIZZARD

NOVEMBER 12, 1940, *MINNEAPOLIS MORNING TRIBUNE*

*T*he forecast for Armistice Day 1940, as reported in the Morning Tribune *dated November 11, gave barely a hint of what was to come that day: "Cloudy, occasional snow, and colder, much colder."*

Many Minnesotans took advantage of the mild holiday weather and made plans to spend the day outdoors. But conditions began to deteriorate after lunch. First came rain… which turned to snow, accompanied by howling wind…and more snow…and then cold, bitter cold. More than sixteen inches of snow fell in Minneapolis and more than two feet in other parts of the state. Temperatures dropped from near sixty degrees to the single digits in less than twenty-four hours. Telegraph and telephone lines went down, cutting off communications and complicating the task of reporting the big story. In the end, forty-nine people died in the Armistice Day blizzard in Minnesota, many of them duck hunters trapped in remote bottomland along the Mississippi River when the blizzard hit.

The Morning Tribune's *"6 A.M. Alarm Clock Edition" of Tuesday, November 12, 1940, provided exhaustive coverage. Here is the lead story:*

N.W. STORM RAGES ON
FORECAST GIVES NO HINT OF LETUP; 7 DIE AS ZERO WAVE RIDES
BLIZZARD
MOTOR TRAFFIC PARALYZED; SCORES OF TOWNS ISOLATED
GALE HITS HARD AT TELEGRAPH AND TELEPHONE SERVICES—AUTO
MISHAPS TRAP 100 NEAR NEW BRIGHTON—BLOCKED STREETS SEND
HUNDREDS TO HOTELS

The Armistice day blizzard that virtually paralyzed transportation and crippled wire communications in Minneapolis and the northwest, roared into Tuesday with no sign of abating.

The weather bureau offered little comfort with a forecast for today of partly cloudy in the south and west parts of Minnesota, with occasional light snow in the northeast portion; Wednesday; fair and continued cold.

Snow had stopped falling at Bismarck and Grand Forks, N.D., this morning but high winds continued the blizzard conditions of Monday.

The storm, which passed through stages of rain and sleet to a blinding gale of snow, hit telegraph and telephone services hard. Most communities were isolated. Temperatures fell by the hour. At 4 a.m. it was 5 degrees above zero in Minneapolis.

The full extent of casualties will not be known until communications are opened up again, but deaths of six men, three of them hunters, and one woman, were reported last night.

The dead:

Walter Strom, 1700 Hawthorne Av., Soo Line fireman, killed in wreck at Watkins.

Mrs. E.Y. Arnold, 2124 Ann Arbor St., St. Paul, traffic victim.

John C. Johnson, 55, 222 Tenth Av. N.E., died of exhaustion.

Harry S. Mason, 75, 329 South Warwick St., St. Paul, died of exhaustion.

Herbert Junneman, Wabasha, Minn., a hunter.

Theodore H. Geiger, Eau Claire, Wis., a hunter.

Thousands of persons stranded in the loop crowded downtown hotels, taking every available room, and overflowing into dining rooms and lobbies. It was the busiest night hotel men could recall.

During the storm, winds reached a velocity of 60 miles an hour, drifts piled up as high as five feet, and there was a temperature drop to sub-zero depths, Williston and Minot, N.D., and Hot Springs, S.D., reporting 10 below.

Practically every road in Minnesota was blocked early today, the state highway department reported.

Plows were kept off highways because of poor visibility, and the danger of accident, but officials said every effort would be made this morning to open up the travel lanes.

Only the tops of cars are visible in this view of snowbound Excelsior Boulevard, looking west toward the Minikahda Golf Club overpass in Minneapolis. *From the* Minneapolis Star Journal.

MOTORISTS WARNED

Meanwhile, they warned motorists not to venture forth unless they had specific and authentic information about road conditions. Those who had found shelter were urged to stay there until conditions improved. Plans were made to send out bulletins on the radio this morning.

STORM CAUSES TRAIN WRECK

Blanketing out visibility by the storm caused a train wreck on the Soo line at Watkins, Minn., in Meeker county, west of Minneapolis. Passenger train No. 106 coming into Minneapolis from Enderlin, N.D., overran a switch signal and collided head on with a freight train. Fireman Strom on the freight train was killed and Engineer Floyd Terpening, 2408 Central Av. N.E., was seriously injured. Two other trainmen were injured.

One woman was killed and her husband and another woman were hurt when their car apparently was thrown into the path of an oncoming truck by the strong winds near the Ramsey county line on highway No. 212. The fatality victim was Mrs. Arnold. Mr. Arnold and Mrs. Nels Chamberlain, 139 East Winnifred St., St. Paul, were taken to Mounds Park hospital. The truck was traveling about 15 miles an hour when the crash came, Mrs. Arnold being thrown out as a door of the automobile was sprung open.

NEARLY 100 MAROONED

Nearly 100 persons, a dozen of them cut by flying glass, were marooned near New Brighton following a mass traffic accident in which 30 or more cars piled into each other on highway No. 8.

Ramsey county deputy sheriffs, with one of them injured in the mixup, helped to get the motorists to New Brighton, while others found refuge in a farmhouse. One of the sheriff's squad cars was almost demolished as it got caught in the crash of cars.

Snowdrifts buried cars along Highway 8 near New Brighton. *From the* Minneapolis Star Journal.

The jam started when an automobile collided with a White Bear–Stillwater bus. Three more cars piled into the bus, and one of them sideswiped an oncoming car in the opposite traffic lane. Within a short time two dozen other motorists, blinded by the snow, slid into the pile of disabled machines. The injured deputy, Kermit Hedman, was severely cut below the knee.

PEDESTRIAN COLLAPSES

Johnson collapsed while walking at University Av. N.E. and Broadway. Passersby carried him to a nearby filling station, where he died a few minutes later. Dr. A.N. Russeth, deputy coroner, said death was due to a heart attack, brought on by exhaustion.

Mason, a retired St. Paul police lieutenant, was found dead in the garage of his home. He apparently died of over-exhaustion while digging tulip bulbs to keep them from freezing. He was found by his daughter, Mrs. John W. McBride, with whom he lived.

Junneman, 38, a barber of Wabasha, Minn., drowned in the Mississippi while he was hunting with several companions. The boat was capsized by the storm. He clung to the side of the overturned craft for awhile, but became numb and exhausted and slipped into the icy water when rescuers were stalled in attempts to reach him.

The bodies of Geiger, 30, and Detra, 34, both of Eau Claire, Wis., were washed up on the shore of the Mississippi river seven miles north of Alma, Wis., last night, victims of the violent snow and windstorm. The men apparently had been hunting ducks in the vicinity.

DUCK HUNTERS MAROONED

Hundreds of Holiday duck hunters were marooned—100 along the Mississippi river between Winona and Wabasha, and another 100 near Parkers Prairie, in addition to smaller parties in various sections. One group on an island near Winona was rescued by a government tow boat.

In Minneapolis, where the rush hour of automobile traffic late in the day packed ice into the ruts of trolley rails, street cars were practically at a standstill by nightfall. Every available plow, 17 in the Twin Cities, of which 11 were in Minneapolis, got on the job, but the fact that nearly 40 street cars were of tracks in various parts of the city served to stall the plows, too. Under the direction of Fred Bjorck,

Rescue workers carried out the body of one of three St. Paul hunters who had taken a boat onto North Lake near Red Wing. *From the* Minneapolis Star Journal.

general superintendent of the Twin City Lines, an all-night fight was made to open up street car traffic.

Early today Mr. Bjorck said it appeared likely that most lines would be open to the public in time to get to work today.

PACK ICE INTO TRACKS

Not only did motorists pack ice into the streetcar tracks, but in some instances, motorists who got stalled on tracks locked their cars and abandoned them. Ice on trolley wires also served to handicap the service.

In the effort to open up the lines, Mr. Bjorck made arrangements to hire a number of city trucks to help the streetcar company. These, in turn, supplemented a fleet of private trucks hired by the company.

Streetcar busses were blocked as well as the street cars by the traffic jam, and by icy hills.

GAMES CALLED OFF

The storm came on a holiday, when schools were closed. Holiday football games between prep school teams were called off, and Armistice day ceremonies, including a parade in Minneapolis, were curtailed or cancelled entirely.

In Minneapolis, the prevailing wind was 27 miles an hour from the northwest, though gusts at times reached 40 to 50 miles. By 7 p.m., the moisture brought by rain and snow measured 2.13 inches in a 24-hour period. There was a high temperature of 38 degrees at 3 a.m. yesterday and then throughout the day and the night, the mercury fell steadily.

COMMUNICATIONS HARD HIT

The fact that telephone and telegraph service was hard hit added to the isolation of various communities of the northwest. Towns were cut off from towns and farms from farms. Scores of communities were able to grope about only within their own immediate snowbound areas and could only surmise what was going on in other places.

Heading to the store for groceries was still a major undertaking even after the snow stopped falling. *From the* Minneapolis Star Journal.

The storm brought special handicaps to various services.

Power company officials, fighting to restore lines, were hampered by road and street conditions, which made use of trucks and automobiles nearly impossible. It was difficult, too, because of the condition of communications, to locate fallen wires.

It was the worst November storm in years, and it was all the more demoralizing because it marked a swift turn from rain to snow, with little warning. Railroads, street car companies and other transportation agencies were caught by surprise and were not immediately prepared to muster equipment and crews. That gave the storm quite a headstart.

Then, too, because of poor visibility and the danger of accidents, snowplows were kept off the highways in many sections.

The Milwaukee railroad's westbound transcontinental Olympian train, which left Minneapolis at 9:25 a.m., got as far as Bird Island, Minn., 98 miles west of Minneapolis, where it was tied up because broken wires interfered with the dispatching system. From their car windows, the passengers watched the drifts pile up around them.

A dozen other trains were either halted or slowed down.

FLOWER FEUD IN EXCELSIOR

MAY 11, 1944, *MINNEAPOLIS TRIBUNE*

*A*s World War II ground on, a story about a flower dispute between two neighbors landed on the front pages of the two Minneapolis dailies. Signe Erickson of Excelsior sued her neighbor, an Excelsior police officer, for $5,000 for false arrest after she was hauled to jail wearing only a coat, a slip and slippers on a cold November night. Her alleged crime? Pouring salt on his flowers. (Both raised flowers for sale.) After a judge cleared her of that disorderly conduct charge, she took the cop to court—and won a $500 judgment. The tears she shed on the witness stand probably swayed the jury. The Tribune captured the scene:

SUING WOMAN STILL WEEPS AS SHE THINKS ABOUT CHILLY ARREST
IN SLIP AND SLIPPERS

Mrs. Signe Erickson of Excelsior still weeps a little when she thinks about how her neighbor, who happened to be an Excelsior police officer, had her arrested on a cold November night last fall when she was dressed only in a slip, slippers and a coat.

She cried a little before District Judge Vince A. Day late Wednesday as trial of her suit against the neighbor, John Kohnkey, Excelsior police officer, for $5,000 for false arrest, got under way.

On the night of Nov. 17, she testified, she had had company. The guests had left, she had washed the dishes and was taking the garbage out to the edge of her lot when she was "grabbed in the back."

Freeman "Dooley" Hoag, acting in Kohnkey's behalf, did the grabbing, she testified.

"He grabbed me and put me in Kohnkey's garage," she said.

Then Kohnkey came, she said, and accused her of pouring salt onto his flowers. Both she and Kohnkey raise flowers for sale.

Kohnkey then put her into his car and took her to the county jail in Minneapolis where she spent the night, she said.

"I asked him if I could go home first," she testified. "I had on only a slip and a coat over it, and he didn't answer me."

She said she was afraid her husband would awaken and, not finding her in bed, might have a heart attack. He had a bad heart, she said.

A friend came to the jail in answer to her pleadings with the jailer that she "wasn't a bum" and arranged to have her released.

At her trial before Justice Tom Bergin, on a complaint by Kohnkey charging her with disorderly conduct, she said Kohnkey testified she had been spreading salt on his garden flowers.

He said, she asserted, that he had found the pan in which she had carried out the garbage, and that it was "sparkling with salt."

There was no salt in the pan when she had it, she declared.

"You can cut my throat if there was," was her testimony.

Justice Bergin was called to the stand to testify from his records that he had acquitted her of the disorderly conduct charge at the trial Nov. 25.

Testimony will continue Thursday.

AERIALIST DIES IN FALL AT STATE FAIR

AUGUST 26, 1947, *MINNEAPOLIS TRIBUNE*

*M*ore than eighteen thousand spectators at the State Fair grandstand were on the edge of their seats. High above the grandstand turf, Lloyd Rellim rode a bicycle back and forth across a narrow bar at one end of a thirty-foot-long metal frame. Another performer twirled on rings and a trapeze bar at the other.

Near the end of the performance, the frame jerked as it was being lowered for Rellim's dismount. He lost his balance and fell seventy-five feet to the ground. Grace Rellim, who was operating the rigging, let out a scream and ran to her husband's side.

"In typical 'the show must go on' fashion," wrote Minneapolis Star *reporter Willmar Thorkelson, "the orchestra struck up a tune and some acrobats started performing. But nobody watched them. We were looking at the bottom of the twin towers where we saw people with flashlights. In a couple of minutes there was an ambulance. As it took Rellim away, its siren drowned out the orchestra."*

The Tribune's *initial account, displayed on page one under an all-caps banner headline, reported that the Rellims' two children—Joyce, eleven, and Neil, five—had witnessed the fatal fall. Neither of them had, it turns out. The sidebar below is a fly-on-the-wall account of their next few hours.*

AERIALIST'S WIFE FACES TRAGIC TASK
MOTHER TO TELL SON DAD IS DEAD

By ED CRANE
Minneapolis Tribune Staff Writer

Today Mrs. Lloyd Rellim is going to have the hardest job of her life. She must tell her son, Neil, 5½, that his father is dead.

Rellim crashed to his death from a 75-foot perch at the Minnesota State fair Monday night.

His daughter, Joyce, 11, burst into uncontrollable tears after the accident, but hours later Neil still did not realize what had happened.

Mrs. Ruth McCrea, who accompanied Rellim to his act, took the two children into her trailer just behind the grandstand, while their mother went to Ancker hospital.

Mrs. McCrea's face was drawn with shock at the sight she could not forget—of Rellim's body toppling past her to smash into the sod. It was drawn, too, with the strain of trying to keep Neil from knowing what had happened.

BOY SEES FIREWORKS

Back of the open-air stage, it was dark, so that tinseled performers, singers, dancers and dwarfs stumbled over guy ropes as they came off stage.

On the other side there were bright lights. Bright lights, a roar of laughter from grandstands that less than an hour earlier had seen a man fall to his death. Lights, laughter and applause.

Backstage, Neil kept pleading with Mrs. McCrea. Finally, at the finale, he won his point. Like other little boys, Neil wanted to see the fireworks. And see them he did.

His tousled, yellow head bent back as rockets zoomed into the sky. His sister, sober-faced, hung in the background.

"Hey, look, Jim," he called to a friend. "Come here, look at Uncle Sam," and he pointed to the fireworks.

There was a bang like an exploding arsenal, and a flash that lit up the whole fairgrounds. Neil didn't wince—his eyes just grew a little bigger, a little rounder.

Once he said, "Mama went away. Why did she go? I wish she could see all this." But a moment later, some new sight had caught his attention.

"I'd like to hold one of those rockets in my hand," he said. And then, as huge globs of yellow fire dripped from the sky, he said, "Gee, I'd like to catch one of those."

From the grandstands came the cries of other children, like Neil, and grownups, too. Backstage, the smoke of the fireworks filled the air and clung to the ground like fog. Biting, acrid smoke that made people's eyes glisten as they watched the youngster.

ALONE IN WORLD

"Everybody's standing in front. I can't see anything," said Neil, and he ran out in front of everybody, out onto the field so that he stood silhouetted against the glare of the dying fireworks—a boy of $5\frac{1}{2}$, standing alone.

The crowd left then, and as the performers hurried off to put away their tinsel and take off their grease paint a car from the sheriff's office drove up. In it rode the woman who today is going to face the hardest job of her life.

I interviewed Joyce (Rellim) Kuhlman, then seventy years old, in August 2006. She still lived in Payson, Illinois, where she and her brother were raised. She remembered her father as a soft-spoken, artistic and mechanically minded man. "I remember setting on his lap at night listening to the radio, Amos and Andy, *curled up in his lap, me on one side and Neil on the other," she said.*

The Rellims spent a lot of time on the road in the 1940s. With his family in tow, Lloyd traveled to forty-two states, Canada and Mexico to entertain audiences. "We had a truck that carried the rigging and a trailer pulled by a car," Joyce said. "It was a LaSalle. It was pretty good size. It was black and it had white sidewalls…We had kind of a shop-like area in the truck, where he had his tools and stuff like that. He could make darn near anything."

Born Lloyd Miller, her father legally changed his name to Rellim—"Miller" spelled backward—when he began performing an aerial act professionally in the late 1920s. He got his start in storybook fashion: "As a kid he ran away with the circus," Joyce said. "He started out as a roustabout and decided that's not what he wanted to do. He wanted to be a performer, so he started training and created a high-wire act." He and three partners worked most frequently with the Barnes-Carruthers Circus.

When World War II began, he lost his partners to the draft. He gave up performing and found work at Higgins Shipbuilding in New Orleans. "They built battleships," Joyce recalled. When the war ended, he offered to perform at the shipyard's victory celebration if the company would build the rigging for a new act he envisioned.

The act was called Blondin-Rellim Cycling in the Sky. Rellim rode a bicycle across a bar at one end of a rectangular frame that pivoted up and down atop a seventy-foot pole. A trapeze artist, Ruth McCrea, performed on rings and a trapeze bar on the opposite end of the frame, about thirty feet away. Rellim's wife, Grace, operated the motorized rigging. "There was no other act like it before or since. He made $100 each time he went up," Joyce said.

To mount the frame, Rellim and McCrea first climbed a ladder and stood on a platform near the top of the pole. "That was the culprit," Joyce said. "There was a hook that caught on the platform and threw him off." Up until a short time before the accident, he had used a safety belt in case of a fall. "But he thought he had perfected the act and was no longer using it," she said. "He never worked with a net."

Joyce, then eleven, was in a grandstand dressing room when she learned of the accident. "Some other show kids came and told me my dad had fallen," she said, but she thought they were joking. "When the adults came and wouldn't let me go outside, I knew something was wrong." Neil hadn't seen the accident, either. "I guess he was down in the dressing room too," she said. She doesn't recall seeing any reporters or photographers.

After the accident, the family returned to Payson to rebuild their lives. Within a year, a Motorola radio factory opened in nearby Quincy, and Grace Rellim got a job there, eventually working as an inspector. Said Joyce, "That's what put us kids through school. She made ninety cents an hour, which was good money at that time."

Lloyd Rellim is buried in Quincy's Greenmount Cemetery. He was first laid to rest in a poorly maintained cemetery in Marion, Illinois, his hometown. But at his widow's request, he was reburied in Quincy within days. "My mother couldn't stand the thought of that old cemetery and the shape it was in," Joyce said. Etched in the granite marker is a picture of his final act, "Cycling in the Sky."

JAILED STRIPPER BLAMES WARDROBE MALFUNCTION

MAY 9, 1953, *MINNEAPOLIS TRIBUNE*

*F*or fans of burlesque, here's a drama in three acts from the Tribune:

STRIPPER STRUTS FROM CITY BAR TO CITY JAIL

Darlene LaBette Varallo, billed as an "esoteric dancer" at the Saddle bar, 415 Hennepin avenue, was "pinched," in a manner of speaking, by the police morals squad Friday night and charged with disorderly conduct.

Miss Varallo, who has been living at the Frederick hotel, 45 E. Fifth street, St. Paul, was arrested at 9:45 p.m. shortly after she finished on the Saddle stage.

IN HER AUDIENCE were Jake Sullivan, head of the morals squad, and two squad members, Robert Smith and Dan Graff.

"It was a lewd and distasteful act," Sullivan said.

He explained that Miss Varallo—billed as an esoteric dancer because police don't tolerate "strip-teasers" in Minneapolis bars—had too little clothing.

All she wore, he said, were a coarse net G-string with fringe and some round plastic objects which Miss Varallo identified as "pasties." (They are held in position with paste.)

THE SQUAD of Sullivan and his two assistants took the "dancer" to city jail as soon as she was properly dressed. Her stage costume—what there was of it—was confiscated as evidence.

Miss Varallo was freed about an hour after her arrest when her employer, A.E. (Eddie) Holman, posted $200 bail. She will answer the charge in police court today.

Before her departure, Miss Varallo told police she is a native of Toledo, Ohio, but has been "dancing" in the Twin Cities about a month, first at the Saddle, then at Heinie's bar in St. Paul, returning a week ago to the Saddle.

Varallo appeared in court the following Thursday. Tribune *reporter Charles W. Bailey, who later became editor of the paper, filed this report:*

CITY STRIPPER GETS TO WEAR THE EVIDENCE
MORALS CHIEF LEFT HOLDING THE ET CETERA

By CHARLES W. BAILEY
Minneapolis Tribune Staff Writer

Two little rhinestone-studded cones, a few lengths of gauze, a fringe and a pair of black net tights had Minneapolis law enforcement circles in a tizzy Thursday.

Darlene LaBette Varallo, an "esoteric" dancer, had the little things first, but she lost them Friday night to Jake Sullivan, head of the police morals squad, for putting on what he called "a lewd and distasteful act."

Sullivan brought them to court yesterday as evidence when Darlene appeared to answer disorderly conduct charges.

HER ATTORNEY, Don Morgan, asked the hearing be put off until today. Then he started the fuss by asking police to loan him the fringe, gauze net, cones, etc., so he could have them photographed in their natural habitat—i.e., on Darlene—to show the court she didn't look "lewd and distasteful" in them.

Judge Luther Sletten said it was all right with him. So did Leo McHale, city prosecutor. Sullivan picked up the fringe, gauze, net, etc., and carried them to the Saddle bar, 415 Hennepin avenue, where Darlene had done the disputed roundelay.

When he got there, though, he balked. He argued with Morgan that there were more lights on when he saw Darlene Friday night.

HE REFUSED to give up the fringe, gauze, etc., unless Darlene would pose for a police cameraman he just happened to have with him.

Darlene Varallo described her dance as a "can-can" plus a mixture of "a shuffle, ball hop, kick, twirls." Police described it as "a lewd and distasteful act." *From the* Minneapolis Tribune.

Morgan said no. Sullivan, trailed by his photographer, deputy inspector Elmer Hart and three morals squad members, went back to his office with the evidence in a paper bag.

Morgan was hot on his heels, claiming his client was being denied her constitutional right to prepare a defense. He hurried to Judge Sletten's chambers. The judge was out.

After waiting three hours for Sletten, Morgan persuaded Judge Betty Washburn to call Thomas R. Jones, police chief. After she told Jones she felt Darlene had a right to pose in the fringe, etc., Jones told Sullivan to take his evidence back in the Saddle again.

This time Sullivan had Fred Tersch, deputy inspector, with him. He gave the paper bag to Darlene. She ducked into her dressing room and returned wearing the et cetera.

"WALK AROUND in a circle," Morgan's photographer told her. She did. Flashbulbs exploded. She went on circling the stage.

"I'm getting dizzy," she complained. Sullivan and Tersch watched the dark-haired dancer impassively. The photographer told her she could go.

Darlene retired, divested herself of the evidence and returned in a less controversial costume. She gave the et cetera back to Sullivan, who claims she wasn't wearing all of it when he arrested her Friday.

Morgan said the whole thing was caused by politics and the impending city election. Eddie Holman, owner of the bar, said it's bad for business. Darlene said she can't sleep nights. Sullivan, left holding the bag, will bring it into court again this morning at 9 a.m.

At her hearing the next day, Varallo blamed the loss of her bra on a wardrobe malfunction, but the judge didn't buy it.

"PEELER" TO APPEAL FINE
"PIVOTS, TWIRLS" FAIL TO SWAY JUDGE

By CHARLES W. BAILEY
Minneapolis Tribune Staff Writer

The Case of the Busted Brassiere (or Where Was the Costume When the Cops Collared the Cutie?) ended—for the time being—in Minneapolis municipal court Friday.

Darlene LaBette Varallo, "esoteric dancer" at the Saddle bar, 415 Hennepin avenue, was fined $100 on a disorderly conduct charge. But Judge Luther Sletten granted a month's stay of sentence to let her attorney, Don Morgan, appeal to the state supreme court. Morgan said he will contest a ruling that a lie detector test given the dancer was not proper evidence.

Before the six hour trial was over, spectators learned a number of things about dancing, costuming, the English language and the lie detector machine.

After Jake Sullivan, Dan Graff and Robert Smith of the police morals squad testified they entered the bar last Friday and watched Darlene do her dance—without a brassiere—Morgan put the dark-haired artiste on the stand to defend herself.

SHE DESCRIBED her dance as a "can-can" plus a mixture of "a shuffle, ball hop, kick, twirls." She denied Sullivan's charge that she had bent over and shaken parts of her anatomy at the audience.

"You can't bend over when you dance or you lose your equilibrium," said Darlene, who testified she has danced since the age of 3 and was an Arthur Murray instructor for two years.

She said she certainly was wearing state's exhibit F (the brassiere) when she began to dance but had to discard it because a strap broke. She also denied removing the state's exhibit E (a tasseled fringe) from its original position around her—ah—middle.

Exhibits A through D include two rhinestone, cone-shaped articles of apparel, one G-string and a pair of black net stockings.

Leo Hale, city prosecutor, asked her if she knew what was meant by the term "esoteric dancer."

"Well, I'm an exotic dancer," Darlene said. "Until yesterday, I thought it was a mistake by the sign painter—that he could not spell.

Downtown Minneapolis in the mid-1950s, looking north from the top of the Foshay Tower. *From the* Minneapolis Tribune.

"Now I think it means a dance for the chosen few. I guess that's because the bar is so small."

"You may be right," McHale said. "I'm no philologist."

"Neither am I!" Darlene retorted, apparently miffed.

"What were you trying to portray?" McHale asked.

"Nothing. I was just trying to entertain the public. Most people can't dance, but everyone has music in his soul."

Morgan also put a series of bar customers and employes on the stand. They testified Darlene was wearing exhibit F when the dance began and that the lights over the stage were dimmer than the police claimed they were.

FINAL WITNESS was Henry Morrison, Jr., a University of Minnesota lie-detector operator. Morgan said he would testify that he had given Darlene a test Thursday night and that she "told substantially the truth." In the questions, Morgan said, Darlene had answered she was wearing exhibit F when she began her dance and did not remove exhibit E.

Judge Sletten refused to admit the test as evidence. After the guilty finding, Morgan said he will appeal the conviction because the test hadn't been allowed as evidence.

SIX KILLED AS JET HITS HOUSE

JUNE 9, 1956, *MINNEAPOLIS STAR*

*O*n Tuesday, June 5, 1956, an Air Force F89 Scorpion fighter jet carrying 104 live rockets crashed into a car on a road adjacent to what is now known as Minneapolis–St. Paul International Airport. A thirty-eight-year-old Minneapolis woman and her five-year-old daughter were killed. Her husband and son escaped from the car before it burst into flames; their housekeeper was seriously injured. The family had been out for a "pleasure ride" to see the new stadium in Bloomington.

Just four days later, an F9F4 jet crashed into a row of homes north of the airport. Here are excerpts from two front-page stories published in the Star on the day of the accident:

JET HITS HOUSE, AT LEAST 6 DEAD
9 INJURED; 5 OTHER HOMES ARE SET AFIRE

A navy jet plane crashed into a house and set fire to five others at the north edge of Wold-Chamberlain field at 9:30 a.m. today, killing at least six persons and injuring nine others.

The plane left a military formation to make an emergency landing and hit the street in front of 5804 and 5808 Forty-Sixth avenue S., near the main gate of the navy base.

The plane then bounced into the home of Donald and Jane Garles, 5820 Forty-sixth, and shattered with a terrific explosion and flash which scattered the plane and its fuel over the neighborhood.

Some 20 or more children were at play in that block when the plane crashed. Some of them were littered with debris and flaming fuel.

The F9F4 jet crashed into a row of homes in the 5800 block of Forty-sixth Avenue South in Minneapolis, just north of Wold-Chamberlain Field, now Minneapolis–St. Paul International Airport. The navy pilot fell short in his attempt to make an emergency landing on a nearby runway. *Earl Seubert,* Minneapolis Tribune.

Five of them, taken to Veterans hospital, were reported in "very critical" condition with burns. One other child was taken to the same hospital with less severe injuries.

Two were taken to General hospital and three to the navy infirmary at the airport.

The pilot of the plane, Major George Armstrong, 33, 5808 Pearson drive, Edina, was killed. The second body identified was that of Debora De Wolfe, 7, 5816 Forty-sixth avenue S.

The child's body was found on a couch in her home. Alongside the couch was the landing gear of the plane.

The other dead were not identified immediately.

Glen Gould, chief of the veterans administration fire department, said six bodies had been recovered.

"We made a pretty close check of the burned homes and I don't believe there are any more," he said.

At a press conference at navy headquarters, Col. Frank F. Gill, commanding officer of the naval air station, explained that Armstrong and two other pilots had taken off on a tactical training mission.

The other two were Maj. O.J. Miller, Isanti, Minn., and Maj. Harold Slay, Somerset, Wis. The three are navy reservists.

Miller, according to Gill, said Armstrong reported he was having some trouble with the plane and was breaking formation to head back to the airport.

"He didn't explain what the trouble was, but he didn't seem to be alarmed," Gill said. "Miller followed him toward the airport.

"Miller said Armstrong appeared to have made the airport and that he, Miller, then turned away from the airport before the crash."…

CHILDREN PLAYING WHEN JET HITS "LIKE A BOMB"
South Minneapolis residents who had been working in their yards, supervising their children at play or going about normal household tasks were shaken at 9:32 a.m. today by an explosion that some described as a "huge bomb blast."

It was the crash of a F9F navy jet fighter plane into a row of houses in the 5800 block on Forty-sixth avenue S. Here are the words of some of the first to reach the scene:

Elmer Gustafson, 5841 Forty-fifth avenue S., was in his back yard when he saw the plane come in low and crash with a "terrific explosion and flash."

Firefighters rushed to extinguish a fire in one of the houses hit by debris. *From the* Minneapolis Star.

"There were lots of youngsters playing in yards just before the crash," he said. "I took my own youngsters a safe distance, then went to the scene of the burning homes. I saw people carrying injured children.

"It was so confusing, I don't know whether the children had been in the houses or in the yard. There was a terrible concussion that could have knocked them over."

Gustafson said he tried to get into one house, but flames drove him back.

Frank Trybulec, Villa Park, Ill., and his wife had just arrived to visit the Albin Andersons at 5759 Forty-fourth avenue S.

"I heard a terrific explosion and I ran to the burning house where the plane had hit," Trybulec said. "They were carrying out children. One child had her clothing burned off."

Mrs. Otto Mueller, 5854 Forty-sixth avenue S., who lives at the far end of the block, spent a frantic minute following the "terrible bang" searching for her children, John, 5½, and Joan, 8, who were playing down the block toward the crash scene.

The two youngsters came rushing into the house. John was scratched by a piece of flying debris, but otherwise unhurt.

Firefighters tended to the grim task of removing the dead. *From the* Minneapolis Tribune.

"Don't come out, Annabelle," Mrs. Mueller telephoned a friend across town as thousands jammed streets, alleys and lawns within minutes after the disaster.

"There was a 'poof' and then a real smell of smoke and I saw fire in my living and bedroom."

Mrs. Doris Kieffer, 30, sat in Veterans' administration hospital after treatment for cuts and described the impact of the jet plane crash that wiped out six houses today.

"I had just gone into the bathroom to comb my hair," she said.

"It is on the west side of the house and the plane hit on the east side.

"I heard the plane and you know jets whistle. But this time it was just a poof and I realized the smell of smoke.

"I saw fire in the living room and bedroom and there is a hall separating it from the bathroom. I started down the hall and realized I couldn't make it.

"I shut the door of the bathroom and broke the bathroom window to get out.

"I saw my two little girls—Jennie, 2½, and Cassie, 5. I got Jennie.

"My husband was painting the back fence and he picked up Cassie.

"We ran across the alley to my neighbor because I knew she was a nurse.

"I said, 'help me, please.'

"Then I saw an ambulance and we took them to it. They were crying. I don't remember much after that."

Mrs. Kieffer had stitches taken in her right forearm and first aid for other less serious cuts and bruises on her legs.

The Kieffers moved into their home four years ago. She said they had never worried about aircraft activity. "It is just one of those things you never think happens," she said.

"After all, the landing strip is over the hill and not really by us.

"You don't worry to the point where you ever think that it would hit you."

LITTLE BOYS TELL A BIG LIE

FEBRUARY 24, 1960, *MINNEAPOLIS STAR*

*H*ey, boys and girls, what's the biggest lie you ever told? The two youngsters in this Minneapolis Star *story got into big trouble when one fed a cop a real whopper. It's straight out of* Leave It to Beaver—*except that they got a good licking instead of a stern lecture in the den.*

SMALL BOYS' FIB GOT OUT OF HAND
OFFICER, A BOY FELL THROUGH THE ICE…WELL, A BOY COULD!

Two small Minneapolis boys got lickings Tuesday for telling a fib to policemen.

It all started when Mark Buchanan, 8, 3115 Clinton Av., and Greg Warren, 7, 3132 Clinton Av., were standing at the edge of a 60-foot embankment gazing at the river at Main St. and SE. 6th Av. about 5 p.m.

Two patrolmen Warren Burns and Matthew J. Trymucha, cruising by in their squad car, noticed the two boys, stopped, and attempted to chase them away.

Mark, however, boldly announced that another boy had "vanished" on the ice, [and] Greg agreed.

Burns slid down the steep bank. Trymucha called for help. More squad cars arrived and the search began. The search was called off a short time later.

But Burns couldn't get back up the bank.

Another call went out, this time for six firemen to rescue Burns. With their help, he climbed up a long rope, cutting his hand in the process.

Mark and Greg were taken to police headquarters. They admitted the whole thing was a fib.

Mark was placed in the juvenile jail for a few hours and was taken home by his mother about 11:30 p.m.

"He'll look you straight in the eye and tell you all sorts of little lies," his mother said, "but he's never done something as big as this before."

She said Mark got a "hard licking with a belt" and was hustled off to bed.

Greg's mother, Mrs. June Warren, said Greg "was scared" when she arrived at police headquarters to retrieve her son.

"He wanted to go home. He said he was sorry. We talked it over, he got a spanking, and I sent him to bed."

Mark explained:

"I start telling stories. I tell a lot of stories, and they sort of get away from me. I get in too deep, and then I can't get out."

CITIES OUT OF SYNC

MAY 10, 1965, *MINNEAPOLIS STAR*

*F*or two weeks in 1965, you had a pretty good excuse for missing a bus or being late for work in Minneapolis and St. Paul. The two cities could not agree when to start daylight saving time. State law designated May 23 as the day to turn clocks forward. St. Paul City Council decided to make the move on May 9, in line with most of the rest of the nation. Minneapolis decided to go by state law and fell an hour behind St. Paul on the second Sunday in May. It was a mess, but people muddled through. The Star story below describes some of the complications.

A year later, Congress stepped in and passed the Uniform Time Act of 1966, establishing a system of uniform times within each of the four time zones in forty-eight states.

CONFUSION REIGNS AS ST. PAUL GOES ON DST

St. Paul was on "wrist watch time" today.

That was really the only way you could be sure of the time in this city, which went on daylight saving time (DST) Sunday morning, two weeks ahead of Minneapolis and much of the rest of Minnesota.

Most business places moved their clocks ahead one hour, but some remained on standard time and moved the starting times of their employes ahead one hour.

All state federal offices, however, were on standard time. The Ramsey County Board opened its regular weekly meeting at 10 a.m. standard time.

The telephone company was still giving out standard time in its recorded time-of-day message.

For two weeks in May 1965, the clock atop Minneapolis City Hall said one thing and the clocks in St. Paul quite another. *From the Minneapolis Tribune.*

Sewage rolled into the Minneapolis St. Paul Sanitary District plant from St. Paul on daylight time, but left on standard time.

If you called a cop, he arrived to take care of your problem on standard time. But if you needed a fireman, he showed up on daylight time.

Two St. Paul policemen arrived for work wearing a wrist watch on each arm, one for standard time and one for daylight time.

Mail arrived an hour earlier at St. Paul homes because the post office is on standard time.

STAGGERED SHIFTS

All city and county offices in which records with deadline times are filed staggered the shifts of some employes to remain open from 7:20 a.m. standard time to 4:30 p.m. daylight time.

Most St. Paul business firms reported little confusion with employes arriving late—or early—for work.

Two clocks were set up at the Northwest Orient Airlines registration desk to aid employes in informing passengers about flight times. Warren Phillips of the United Airlines desk said, "We just ask people what time it shows on their watch and give them directions according to that."

Al Olson, St. Paul City Council recorder, probably had the best solution. "I don't have any watch," he said. "I'm going to work when I'm hungry."

BURIED ALIVE IN BLOOMINGTON

JUNE 29, 1965, *MINNEAPOLIS STAR*

More than forty-five years ago, JeanMarie Louise Frazier found herself buried alive in a storm-sewer excavation near her Bloomington home. She survived with hardly a scratch, thanks to quick thinking on the part of her little sister, three neighbors and a construction worker. Her story landed on the front page of the Star *the next day:*

"LIKE GOPHERS"
MEN DIG TO SAVE BURIED GIRL

"My sister's in the hole…my sister's in the hole…"

This alarm, sounded quick and loud by 5-year-old Suzan[ne] Frazier, 8308 17th Av. S., Bloomington, produced a chain reaction about 8 p.m. Monday.

Tony Koval, 15, 8313 17th Av. S., who was fixing his fence, saw the girl running across the street from a storm sewer excavation.

Koval understood. He dropped his hammer and ran toward the excavation shouting for help at the same time.

Raymond C. LeValley, 8301 17th Av. S., dropped his newspaper and raced through his front door. Bruce Swenson, 8337 17th Av. S., was talking to Marvin Goulet, 580 Holly Av., St. Paul, a contractor's man keeping an eye on a pump.

The two men broke into a sprint. By the time they and LeValley reached the spot, Koval had discovered a speck of Jeanmarie Louise

Frazier, 8, almost completely buried by an earth cave-in inside the excavation.

"First I saw a hand, then I could see her eyes," Koval said.

The four men got down on their knees and dug with their hands "like gophers," releasing the girl before emergency equipment arrived.

Jeanmarie, flustered and frightened, ran home unhurt.

In a 2008 interview, JeanMarie explained what happened: Mrs. Harold Frazier had forbidden her children to go near the excavation that summer. How did JeanMarie end up in that hole, buried alive by a cave-in, unable to breathe, her nose, mouth and throat filling with dirt?

"I never obeyed my mother," said JeanMarie Rosenthal, who was then fifty-one and living in St. Paul. "I was a very stubborn child. I always wanted to do my own thing. My daughter is actually the same way."

And so JeanMarie and Suzanne found themselves on the edge of the sewer-line excavation that night, throwing rocks into the hole, when suddenly the earth gave way and swallowed the older child, covering all but her right arm. At least, that's the way JeanMarie remembered it in our initial interview.

But memory is a funny thing. She called me back thirty minutes later to set the record straight after consulting by phone with her sister, who was then forty-nine and living in Bloomington. What really happened won't surprise any parent—or any kid: the two children had climbed into the hole to play. On the way back up, JeanMarie grabbed onto a root that came loose and started the cave-in that buried her.

"I couldn't hear anything," she recalled. "I just remember thinking, 'I'm gonna die, help!'"

Luckily, Suzanne made it to safety. But she didn't shout, "My sister's in the hole! My sister's in the hole!" Like many five-year-olds, she had trouble with the word "sister." What she shouted was, "My scissors in the hole! My

The Frazier girls looked appropriately guilty in this image from *Minneapolis Star* microfilm.

scissors in the hole!" She ran home to get her mother as three neighbors and a workman raced to save her sister.

"I could feel movement above me, so I knew that there was somebody up there," JeanMarie said. "I think it was a miracle that my arm was even up there, because if that hadn't been there they wouldn't really know where I was."

The men dug frantically and pulled her out. A neighbor told her she'd been buried for about three minutes. Another three minutes without oxygen and she would have suffered brain damage.

Mr. Koval, one of the neighbors, helped her home. Her mother, alerted by Suzanne's shouting, met her in the street. "She hugged me at first to make sure that I was okay," JeanMarie said. And then? "I'm sure I got a scolding," she said.

THE BIG LAKE ONE

FEBRUARY 25, 1966, *MINNEAPOLIS STAR*

I'm not sure what caught my attention about this story, which appeared under a two-column headline on an inside page of the Star. Maybe it was the year: 1966 seemed early for a Vietnam-era draft protest. More likely it was the reference to "two buckets of human excrement" in the first paragraph.

Barry Bondhus, the youth arrested in connection with the protest more than forty-five years ago, was working as a toolmaker/machinist in Princeton, Minnesota, when I called him in 2008. Did he have time for a phone interview about this period in his life? Yes, he said, but he added that the event was probably bigger than I realized and that I'd likely need more than a phone call to capture the full story. He mentioned that his father had declared war on the United States and that the government, in effect, surrendered. And without elaborating, he said that excrement was chosen as a protest tool for a specific reason.

He mailed me several documents about his protest, arrest and conviction. A subsequent interview with him follows the original news story.

"FLAG-DRAPED CASKETS"
YOUTH, 20, ARRESTED AFTER DRAFT PROTEST

A 20-year-old Big Lake youth was being held in Hennepin County Jail under $10,000 bond today on a charge that he dumped two buckets of human excrement into the files of the Sherburne County draft board [in Elk River].

Held is Barry Bondhus, who was arrested by FBI agents Thursday night at his home.

He is one of 12 children of Thomas Bondhus, 43, who operates machine shops at Big Lake, Monticello and Orrock in Sherburne County.

Sidney Abramson, assistant U.S. district attorney, said the youth would be given a hearing today before U.S. Commissioner Bernard Zimpfer in Minneapolis Federal Court.

The arrest of the youth apparently climaxed a series of difficulties he and his father have had with the draft board.

The elder Bondhus said he has told the board repeatedly that he is opposed to any of his sons serving in the armed forces.

"If you draft Barry I have nothing to look forward to for the next 24 years but flag-draped caskets," he said.

Barry is the second oldest of 10 Bondhus boys.

After a board hearing Feb. 15, the youth was classified 1-A and ordered to take a pre-induction physical examination in Minneapolis.

The FBI said the youth refused to cooperate.

Wednesday, the complain charged, young Bondhus walked into the board's office and dumped the substance into six draft board file cases. His draft board status still is pending.

A fat manila envelope filled my mail slot at work about a week after Barry Bondhus and I first spoke on the phone in 2008. It contained a cover letter detailing his protest, arrest and conviction; a term paper about the event written by his youngest daughter while she was in high school; his father's "declaration of war" against the United States; a one-page explanation of why human excrement was used in the protest; and a copy of a song about him that was part of an antiwar play performed in England.

Here's what I've pieced together about "the Big Lake One," as Barry Bondhus came to be known:

Soon after Barry received his draft notice in 1965, his father, Tom, composed the fiery declaration of war. He showed the missive to friends and family but apparently didn't intend it for a wider audience. Perhaps he was blowing off steam or outlining his arguments for a later meeting with the draft board. At any rate, Tom Bondhus's mother mailed the two-page, single-spaced document to the government without her son's knowledge. "His mother was a little bit strange about things," Barry recalled. "They used to argue about the Bible."

A few key passages from Tom's declaration:

- *"Most people agree that war accomplishes nothing. I have asked myself from the beginning; Why go to war? When I was of draft age in the...second world war, I was constantly afraid of being forced into the army; not because I was afraid to*

Tom and Barry Bondhus stood together in opposing military conscription. "If you draft Barry I have nothing to look forward to for the next 24 years but flag-draped caskets," Tom Bondhus told the draft board. *Pete Hohn, Minneapolis Tribune.*

die, but because I would refuse to kill others that were no more guilty than myself. The boys don't deserve to die for the bungling of the politicians."

- *"My opinion is that since our constitution guarantees: Life, Liberty, and The Pursuit of Happiness; and because the army denies all three; the draft is not lawful."*

- *"God is not with us, we will never win another war, the trend is over for us. Our Boys fought valiantly in Korea with many men and much material, against a very small, weak adversary, and after a long struggle it was a draw. We attacked Cuba and were driven off."*

- *"You are like filthy swine that eat the flesh of your own children. You worship false gods. You have sunk to the lowest form of life as described in the Bible."*

Then it gets, well, intense:

"I therefore state my terms: My boy will not be available for the draft, on my orders as his father. He is a 'MINOR and responsible to me, and me for him, and he is obligated to obey me. His orders are not to come, so your quarrel is with me. If anyone comes to take my boy, you must be prepared to Kill Me. I will meet whoever comes on my front door step with a single shot, shot gun, and will attempt to kill the first man that gets in my house. I will have only one shot in the gun, and after I kill the man I will surrender, AS A PRISONER

OF WAR. You will have a chance to kill me anytime before I kill your man as I will use No. 6 shot with a killing range of less than 50 feet."

He concluded:

"None of my children has ever troubled the law because, I have taught them to obey the law, I have also taught them to love God, and hate the military...The reason my children love me is because I love them, and will fight and die for them if necessary...My terms are not unreasonable: the government must not take my children. If you want money or property, take it, but you cannot use my children to do your fighting. Fight your own war You Cowards."

The declaration mentions "the Law of Moses" and "God's law" and cites Jeremiah 10:21. What role did religion play in the family? "My dad tried a lot of religions and never did get along with any of them," Barry said. "He actually started his own church before all this. I was ordained a minister. Church of the Morning Star, we called it," after seeing a bright star in the sky during the trial.

Barry said that his dad, a machinist, admired guns and "owned lots" of them. He didn't hunt much as an adult but had a pistol range in the basement.

The declaration's threat of force explains why we need to go on the record at this point with a belated correction. Bondhus was arrested at the Sherburne County attorney's office, not at his Big Lake home, as reported in the Star. *Government agents weren't exactly eager to appear at the Bondhuses' front door. Here's what happened:*

"Almost a week after I dumped the residue in the files...my dad received a phone call from the Sherburne County Attorney stating there were two men from the government in his office that would like to talk with us. My father and I went to his office in Elk River to meet with them. After talking to them for about an hour they told us they were from the FBI and showed us they were armed and at that time they arrested me. The county attorney told my dad that the FBI told him that the reason they had not arrested me earlier was because of my father's Declaration Of War (copy enclosed). No one from the FBI was willing to go to Big Lake."

Barry Bondhus was charged with destruction of government property and interfering with the Selective Service Administration. He was tried and convicted in December 1966. He was sentenced to eighteen months in jail and fined $2,500. He served fourteen months in a series of jails and prisons: Madison, Wisconsin; Milan, Michigan; Peoria, Illinois; Leavenworth, Kansas; and finally Sandstone, Minnesota. With time off for good behavior, he was released in March 1968.

What about the excrement? Let's back up to February 1966, when Barry Bondhus and his parents visited the local draft board to discuss his classification. Tom Bondhus explained that, as the father of ten sons, he "naturally would be more concerned and more emotional about losing his boys to the army" than a person with only one boy. The chairman of the draft board responded with a kind of wisecrack: "You have ten boys, do you. Where's the rest of them?"

That didn't sit well with Tom Bondhus, who seethed over the next few days, considering responses that ranged from "cutting open a certain Pig to see if he had a heart" to "moving to a peace loving country where the boys wouldn't be forced to serve in an army of aggression."

"Finally," Barry Bondhus wrote, "an old sage in the family pointed out that when an ass hole makes a statement, it must have been shit he was talking about; so we concluded that by the rest of the Bondhus boys, he meant the residue...Therefore it was decided that no one could be so [foul] as to ask for all of the boys themselves; he must have meant [their residue]."

So the Bondhus boys began collecting their waste in a stainless steel cream can in the bathroom "for a week or so," Barry recalled. "It was starting to get a little rank by the end." The residue was then

December 2, 1966: Tom Bondhus outside the federal courthouse in Minneapolis, with a book open to Washington's farewell address. *Dwight Miller,* Minneapolis Tribune.

transferred to two "dirty old tar buckets" for a one-way trip to Elk River.

Barry's daughter Sandi, in her high school paper, picks up the story from there:

"He took the two buckets to the draft board office in Elk River...and set them on the secretary's desk. He then asked, 'Here's the rest of my brothers[;] what do you want me to do with them?' She was so scared she just kept repeating, 'I don't know what you're talking about.' My dad then commented, 'Well, if you don't know what to do with them I'll put them in here.' He opened up the top drawer of the draft filing cabinets and poured the two buckets in them. Then he quickly shut each one so the residue would run down and ruin all of the draft papers in that office." Damage was estimated at $500.

"While I was in jail," Barry Bondhus wrote in his letter to me, "my father met with Miles Lord [a freshly minted U.S. district judge at the time]. On behalf of the U.S. Government he promised my father that they would never draft any of his sons. This is the kind of thing you wouldn't expect them to put in writing...but...the government has never tried to draft any of his sons. We interpret this as a victory in the war he declared on the government. My father was never charged with any crime."

BURNING MONEY TO SURVIVE

FEBRUARY 2, 1971, *MINNEAPOLIS TRIBUNE*

Jim Marshall of the Minnesota Vikings and Minneapolis Star *columnist Jim Klobuchar were among sixteen snowmobilers who set out from Red Lodge, Montana, for a fifty-five-mile mountain ride to Cooke via Beartooth Pass one morning in late January 1971.*

Conditions were fine at the start, but by afternoon, winds had begun to rise, with gusts up to one hundred miles per hour. Blowing snow reduced visibility to nothing, and wind chills dropped to eighty below zero. One by one, the machines began to fail and were abandoned. The party broke into smaller groups and sought shelter on foot. Hugh Galusha, fifty-one, president of the Minneapolis Federal Reserve Bank, and another man built a snow shelter along the highway. But it wasn't enough: by 7:00 a.m., Galusha was dead, the victim of exposure.

In an interview with Tribune *columnist Sid Hartman a few days later, Marshall recounted his tale of survival:*

MARSHALL BURNED MONEY TO KEEP ALIVE ON TREK

By SID HARTMAN
Minneapolis Tribune Staff Correspondent

Jim Marshall had to burn his money to stay alive. The Minnesota Viking defensive end, one of a party of 16 that was stranded in deep snow during a blizzard on Beartooth Pass, Wyo., gave his account of the trip that cost the life of Hugh Galusha, 51, president of the Minneapolis Federal Reserve Bank.

As conditions deteriorated, Jim Marshall's sled hit a snow ridge and slammed into a guardrail, pitching him over the rail. He rolled down the slope for thirty feet before he managed to dig his feet and fingers into the loose rock, averting a two-thousand-foot fall to the bottom of the canyon. This photo, filed without caption information in the *Star Tribune* library, would appear to be Marshall's sled, based on several newspaper accounts published in February 1971.

"After we were stranded, we walked from about noon Saturday until about 2:30 a.m. Sunday morning before we found a place we felt would provide suitable shelter," said Marshall on his return to Minneapolis Monday night.

"Before my snowmobile quit operating, I had a narrow escape when my machine went over a cliff and almost rolled on top of me.

"There was a 2,000-foot drop at the spot of my accident. After I had dropped about 30 feet, I was lucky enough to be able to grab on to some rock. Then with the aid of some of the other members of our party I was pulled back to safety."

Marshall said that he, Paul Dickson (Viking tackle) and Bob Leiviska Jr. and Vern Waples, the guide on the trip and his wife, had started walking with the idea of reaching a place called Top of the World—a store and motel in the area that is frequented by tourists in the summertime—after their machines quit operating.

"It got to be dark and we were afraid to stop for fear we would freeze to death.

"The snow reached the waist of Dickson and myself. The lighter people could walk on top of the snow and not get stuck. Paul and I would take three or four steps and we'd be worn out.

"We passed about three or four stages of total exhaustion before we finally decided we couldn't go any farther.

"Finally, young Leiviska (15 years old) located a piece of land with a grove of trees and a hill in back of it to block the wind. We decided to try and stay there for the night.

"The snow was about 10 to 15 feet deep in this area.

"Dickson took out his lighter and we started the fire with five one-dollar bills, some candy wrappers, my checkbook and billfold.

"The snow melted, giving us a hole about six feet deep by eight feet wide.

"Dickson had some $20 bills to keep the fire going.

"Money didn't mean anything at this stage," Marshall said. "You can't beat nature with money. We would have burned everything we had if necessary.

"We kept the fire going with any wood which would burn, including boughs and pine cones. We also stripped the low branches of 15 to 20 trees.

"We were afraid if we went to sleep we might freeze to death. You'd get that warm feeling with a strong desire to go to sleep. You had to work hard to stay awake. You'd stop shivering. You felt so good you wanted to lay down. It was a tough battle to stay awake.

"We were sure at the time that nobody else in the party had survived.

"Sunday morning Mrs. Waples and Leiviska left to try and get help.

"When help hadn't reached us about an hour before dark Sunday night, Dickson and I decided it would be unwise to spend another night in the open.

"We walked about a mile, and saw some snow vehicles that had come to pick us up. You can't imagine how happy we were.

"We also finally got reunited with the rest of the party."

Marshall described the experience as "the toughest thing I've ever encountered in my life."

As one of the Minnesota Vikings' famed Purple People Eaters, Marshall was no stranger to the elements. Here, he drew a bead on Terry Metcalf of the St. Louis Cardinals during a playoff game at Metropolitan Stadium in Bloomington on December 21, 1974. *From the Minneapolis Tribune.*

The star Viking didn't think his physical condition had anything to do with his survival. "It was more the lessons of determination and competition one learns in football that helped me the most.

"I never worked so hard in my life to stay alive. It reached a point where I thought it was virtually impossible to go on. Yet I was able to catch my second, third and fourth wind and go on another two or three miles when the going was the toughest. This is where football helped."

Marshall and his group went some 36 hours without food or water except for a couple of candy bars and a small piece of salami.

"I'm going into the hospital for a week to get my body back in shape," said Marshall. "But I'd go back and try again if I could get myself in condition."

SKINNY - DIPPER LANDS IN COURT

AUGUST 8, 1975, *MINNEAPOLIS TRIBUNE*

*W*hile *scrolling through a roll of* Tribune *microfilm from August 1975, I found news pages dotted with references to a severe shortage that sparked hoarding and theft across the land. The crisis prompted a Richard Guindon cartoon and, in Canada, at least one heated confrontation in the halls of government.*

Can you guess which product or commodity was in short supply that summer?

> *a. gasoline*
> *b. Levi's jeans*
> *c. canning lids*
> *d. toilet seats*

The answer follows this completely unrelated but hilarious/disturbing Tribune *story about a young skinny-dipper's run-in with a stern judge in Hennepin County.*

Man Who Swims without Suit Faces One

By Linda Picone
Staff Writer

How do you explain to a stern-faced judge just why you felt like going skinny-dipping in a city lake one night?

"Why didn't you have a bathing suit?" asked Hennepin County Municipal Judge C. William Sykora.

"I just forgot it," answered Frederick S. Engen, 24.

Hennepin County municipal judge C. William Sykora.

It wasn't the right answer.

"Do you want to get yourself 30 days in the workhouse? You just got it," said Judge Sykora. "There's nothing I like less than a smart aleck. Now, why didn't you wear a bathing suit?"

"I just didn't," said Engen.

Again the wrong answer. Judge Sykora sentenced Engen to 30 days in the workhouse and the bailiff led him out of the courtroom. Other defendants in the courthouse squirmed. If Engen got 30 days for swimming in the nude, what kind of sentences did they face for breach of the peace or simple assault?

But when court recessed shortly after Engen was led out of the room, Judge Sykora told the bailiff, "When that kid on the swimming bit gets sufficiently excited about being here, don't take him over there (to the jail), bring him back."

A chastened Engen came back into the room and Judge Sykora asked him what he had learned. One thing he had learned, Engen said, was that he didn't want to go to jail. Judge Sykora asked him once again why he didn't have a suit, and Engen tried to explain that he had never swum in the nude before and he wanted to try it but he was sure sorry he had.

"The first responsibility every young person has to learn is responsibility for taking care of himself," said Judge Sykora. "That means not being a smartass."

Engen still has a 30-day workhouse sentence facing him, but Judge Sykora stayed it for a year, on the condition that Engen not get picked up for anything worse than a parking ticket during that time.

Another swimmer, pleading guilty to swimming in an unauthorized area (his second offense), came off only slightly better. When he tried to explain that he thought the law was silly and that's why he kept on breaking it, Judge Sykora said, "Why don't you go over to Russia?

Here the theory is that the majority of the people make the law and the rest obey the law."

The swimmer got a $10 fine and a nod from Judge Sykora. "Sorry to give you a lecture," said the judge. "I should have charged you more just for that."

A man with rubbish on two lots was given two weeks to clean it up or face 60 days in the workhouse. "It's 60 days if you don't clean them up, 30 if you clean up one and not the other and nothing if you clean them both," said Judge Sykora. "That's what we call extortion."

The answer to the shortage question is (c) canning lids.

THE CONGDON MURDERS

JUNE 28, 1977, *MINNEAPOLIS TRIBUNE*

*L*umber and mining heiress Elisabeth Congdon, eighty-three, and her night nurse, Velma Pietila, were slain at the Congdon mansion in Duluth in June 1977. Congdon's daughter, Marjorie Caldwell, and her husband, Roger Caldwell, were soon charged with the murders. In a plea deal, Roger Caldwell confessed to second-degree murder in the killings and served five years of a twenty-year sentence. Marjorie Caldwell was acquitted in a 1979 trial.

Roger killed himself in 1988, leaving behind a suicide note asserting his innocence in the murders. Marjorie was later implicated in other deaths and served time in Minnesota and Arizona prisons in separate arson cases.

DULUTH WOMAN, NURSE SLAIN

By Peg Meier and Joe Kimball
Staff Writers

Elisabeth Congdon, 83 years old and one of Minnesota's richest people, was found slain in a bed of her Duluth mansion early Monday morning, a pillow smothering her face.

Her nurse, Valma [*sic*] Pietila, also was killed in the 39-room house. She had been beaten over the head with an 8-inch brass candlestick and died in a pool of blood on a stairway landing.

Duluth police said last night they had no suspects in the case, which has all the elements of the opening chapters in an Agatha Christie mystery. Inspector Ernie Grams said the motive apparently was robbery. "An empty jewelry box was on the floor of the bedroom and the room was ransacked," he said.

A car stolen from the estate was found yesterday at the Minneapolis–St. Paul International Airport. Authorities were concentrating their investigation on the North Shore of Lake Superior and at the airport during the day yesterday. But by evening they admitted they were back to combing the house and car for clues.

The bodies of the two women were found at 7 a.m. yesterday by a nurse who was to relieve Mrs. Pietila of nursing duties. Miss Congdon had suffered a stroke about 8 years ago and had around-the-clock nursing help. Paralyzed on one side, she was confined to a wheelchair.

A policeman stood watch inside the gated estate. *Darlene Pfister,* Minneapolis Tribune.

A chauffeur and a gardener live on the 7½-acre estate but sleep in servants' quarters in separate buildings, police said. A cook was in the mansion Sunday night; she slept in a different wing from Miss Congdon and Mrs. Pietila. The cook, Prudence Renquist, said she heard no unusual noises during the night. She told police, however, that her poodle started barking at about 3 a.m.

A 7-foot-high fence made of brick and metal surrounds the estate. Two gates were kept padlocked.

Police theorized that the assailant or assailants broke into the house through a rear window in the basement, which they found broken. Mrs. Pietila apparently heard noises and went to investigate. Her bedroom was across the hall from Miss Congdon's. She was hit at least once, and very hard, with the candlestick, police said, and fell down six steps to a landing. She climbed onto or was placed on a window seat on the landing, where she was found.

Blood, apparently Mrs. Pietila's, was found on Miss Congdon's pillow. Police said blood apparently had gotten on the killer, who had then rubbed against the pillow.

Mrs. Pietila had been a regular nurse for Miss Congdon until May, when she retired at age 65. Her husband said she was asked to work Sunday night to fill in for a nurse who wanted the night off.

Loren Pietila, her husband, was notified of the slaying and got to the mansion about 8 a.m. He discovered that his wife's car, a 1976 white and tan Ford Granada, was missing. Later in the morning police from the Minneapolis–St. Paul International Airport called him to say his car keys, which had his name attached, were found in an airport trashcan. He told the airport police that the car had been involved in the slayings and asked them to call Duluth police.

Airport police then looked for the car, which they found in the airport parking lot. The state crime lab examined the car for clues yesterday and then impounded it.

A State Patrol helicopter was used to search the 20-mile area between Duluth and Two Harbors. Police officers and dogs combed the estate grounds this morning. The property on Duluth's exclusive London Rd. has hundreds of feet of lakeshore along Lake Superior.

Police had a suspect for a while yesterday, someone children saw

Elisabeth Congdon.

Velma Pietila.

near the mansion. Police, however, found a man matching the suspect's description—white, thin, with long hair and wearing a bluejean jacket—and he had a good reason for being in the area.

Elisabeth Congdon, called "Miss Elisabeth" by many in Duluth, was the last survivor of seven children of Chester A. Congdon, who made millions of dollars in the mining and lumber industries of Minnesota around the turn of the century.

Elisabeth attended Vassar College. As a young woman she was involved in several charities. She was the first president of the King's Daughters Society, which later became the Junior League of Duluth. She was president of the League also.

Chester Congdon, Elisabeth's father, was a prominent lawyer in Duluth whose fortunes rose with the success of northern Minnesota's mining industry.

Before her stroke, she was active in arts and symphony groups and often had people to her house. She attended the First United Methodist Church weekly and often gave flowers grown in her greenhouse to the church. Women from the congregation sometimes held meetings at her home.

People who know her described her as pleasant. "She was very likable," one person said. "All those Congdon girls were, but especially Elisabeth." (She had two sisters.)

She spent winters at her home in Tucson, Ariz., and had another house on the Brule River in northern Wisconsin. Several people expressed surprise yesterday that she was in Duluth rather than Wisconsin the night of the slayings.

Her father was a prime owner of the Oliver Iron Mining Co., which became a subsidiary of U.S. Steel. A conservative Republican, he served in the state Legislature. Congdon died shortly after the 1916 election, and Duluth legend has it that it was of heartbreak because Woodrow Wilson snatched the presidency from Charles Evans Hughes.

Duluth people say Congdon's reputation was less than sterling. "He was a sharpie," said one man who knows the family history.

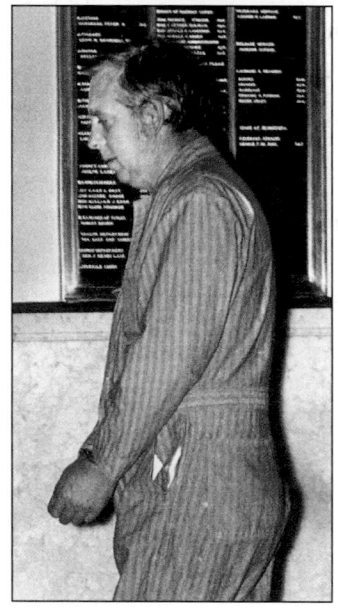

Duluth police quickly turned their attention to Marjorie Caldwell, Congdon's daughter, and Marjorie's husband, Roger Caldwell. Marjorie had a history of extravagant spending, and the couple were known to be in financial straits. *From the* Minneapolis Tribune.

"He was a legal pro who trampled all over people to make money." Another person said of him, "He never opened his purse very wide, but his daughter Elisabeth was very generous."

She gave large sums of money to her church, to the Duluth Symphony, to state arts groups and to local people she heard needed help. One person said, "Some rich people play a brass band every time they give away some money, but she did things quietly. She didn't like publicity." The value of Miss Congdon's estate is hard to estimate, Duluth people said yesterday, but several placed it in the tens of millions.

The family holdings were extensive. The family apparently was once a major investor in the iron mining company now known as the Mesabi Trust. The trust has exclusive rights to about 10,000 acres of land near Babbitt, Minn., much of which is Reserve Mining Company's open-pit mine. For allowing Reserve to mine taconite there, Mesabi receives handsome royalties. The Congdon family, however, is no longer believed to be a major holder of Mesabi Trust certificates.

The family also had large holdings in the Yakima Valley in Washington and held stock in many Midwest corporations.

Although she never married, she did have two adopted daughters, whom she adopted as children.

They are Marjorie Caldwell of Golden, Colo., and Jennifer Johnson of Racine, Wis. Miss Congdon is survived by 13 grandchildren and two great-grandchildren.

The Congdon estate, overlooking Lake Superior, on the morning after the murders. *Darlene Pfister,* Minneapolis Tribune.

In 1970 Miss Congdon's sister-in-law, Dorothy Congdon, who lives a block away on London Rd., shot and killed a 17-year-old youth who police said had broken into her house.

Elizabeth Congdon allowed a movie producer to use her mansion as the filming site of a 1972 movie, "You'll Like My Mother." It was about a murder. A young, pregnant Vietnam widow, played by Patty Duke, goes to visit her dead husband's mother in the family mansion. It seems the mother has been murdered and one of the murderers pretends to be the mother.

Funeral services for Miss Congdon had not been arranged last night.

ABOUT THE AUTHOR

Ben Welter, news copy chief at the *Star Tribune* newspaper, is a Minneapolis native and a graduate of the University of Minnesota. At work, he edits stories and writes headlines and photo captions. In his free time, he fishes for bluegills, rides a mountain bike and plays hockey and Scrabble. His history blog, "Yesterday's News," features stories and photos culled from the Minneapolis newspaper's 145-year-old microfilm archive. To avoid dating himself, he established one rule at the blog's launch in 2005: stories published during his own lengthy newspaper career do not qualify as "Yesterday's News." He has broken that rule just once, posting an account of Twins legend Kirby Puckett's exhausting first day in the Big Leagues in May 1984.

Your comments, memories and suggestions are welcome at www.startribune.com/yesterday. Or follow him on Twitter: @oldnews.